CITIES A.
CREATIVE CLASS

CITIES AND THE CREATIVE CLASS

Richard Florida

Routledge
New York · London

Published in 2005 by
Routledge
270 Madison Avenue
New York, NY 10016
www.routledge-ny.com

Published in Great Britain by
Routledge
2 Park Square
Milton Park, Abingdon
Oxon OX14 4RN U.K.
www.routledge.co.uk

Routledge is an imprint of the Taylor and Francis Group.
Printed in the United Stated of America on acid-free paper.

10 9 8 7 6 5 4

Library of Congress Cataloging-in-Publication Data

Florida, Richard L.
  Cities and the creative class / Richard Florida.
    p. cm.
  Includes bibliographical references and index.
  ISBN 0-415-94886-X (hb : alk. paper) -- ISBN 0-415-94887-8 (pb : alk. paper)
  1. City dwellers. 2. City and town life. 3. Professional employees.
4. Creative ability--Economic aspects. 5. Economic geography. I. Title.
  HT201.F56 2004
  307.76--dc22
                                          2004009276

Table of Contents

ACKNOWLEDGMENTS

This book reflects a decade's worth of research and writing and at least three decades of thinking. A huge number of intellectual debts are accumulated over such a period. I am grateful to have had a series of patient funders who invested in the development of these ideas. In particular, I'd like to thank the Alfred P. Sloan Foundation for supporting my work over the better part of two decades. The Heinz Philanthropies supported my professorship at Carnegie Mellon and a number of key projects. I also benefited from funding from the Richard King Mellon Foundation and the Pennsylvania Technology Investment Authority among other groups. Carnegie Mellon University's Heinz School of Public Policy and Management, and more recently the Software Industry Center, provided a supportive environment in which to conduct this work.

My single largest debt is to my parents, who invested virtually everything they had in my intellectual development, and to my brother, Robert, who was my earliest partner in the process of discovery.

I am hugely indebted to the incredible teachers, professors, and mentors I had the good fortune to come across as a student. Martin Kenney has had the greatest impact on my thinking. Gordon Clark has been a particularly great friend and teacher. Ashish Arora, Wesley Cohen, Harvey Brooks, and Lewis Branscomb helped deepen my understanding of the innovation process. Jane Jacobs has taught me more than I could ever have imagined about the nature of cities and places.

Timothy McNulty has been an ongoing source of insight on economic development.

The work upon which this book is based reflects partnerships with an incredible group of colleagues, collaborators, and graduate students. Gary Gates, with whom I wrote Chapter 6, has taught me much about the importance of tolerance, diversity, and inclusion. Kevin Stolarick has been my partner and right arm in data development. Meric Gertler and Zoltan Acs have been insightful collaborators on several projects. Among an amazing group of recent graduate student colleagues and research assistants, Elizabeth Currid, Derek Davison, Brian Knudsen, Sam Youl Lee, and Irene Tinagli stand out.

I am grateful to Rodgers Frantz and Sarah Gross, my partners in the Creativity Group, for supporting my efforts to communicate my ideas in recent years. Mike Vargo and Jesse Elliott have been of invaluable assistance in helping edit and improve my writing. Susan Schulman is a terrific agent, and David McBride of Routledge an extremely capable editor.

A host of people provided technical support and comments on various chapters. Bruce Katz, Amy Liu, and Ben Margolis provided helpful comments on Chapter 6. Bob Yaro and Chris Jones provided comments on Chapter 8. Campos Market Research conducted the focus groups reported in Chapter 3. I thank the many people who assisted with this research, especially those who organized site visits and participated in interviews and focus groups. Diane O'Toole provided administrative support for much of the period during which this work was conducted.

I am grateful to my family as well as many friends and colleagues, some new and some old, across this country and the world, who support my own creative efforts in so many untold ways. Last but not least, I thank the people I have met and continue to meet in my travels who are working so hard to make the creative age a reality in their communities. Your efforts teach me a great deal, and your energy inspires me to continue to learn more.

1
INTRODUCTION

Cities are cauldrons of creativity. They have long been the vehicles for mobilizing, concentrating, and channeling human creative energy. They turn that energy into technical and artistic innovations, new forms of commerce and new industries, and evolving paradigms of community and civilization. Little is revolutionary in this idea. We have known it intuitively for ages, and its manifestations can be just as easily seen in Athens, Rome, Venice, and Florence, or London, Paris, and Berlin, as in New York, San Francisco, Boston, Seattle, Toronto, Dublin, Helsinki, or Sydney. The argument of this book is not that the role of creativity in city formation and growth is new, but that, with the decline of physical constraints on cities and communities in recent decades, creativity has become *the* principal driving force in the growth and development of cities, regions, and nations.

In a sense, this book represents the prequel to *The Rise of the Creative Class*. Its core chapters are made up of the original academic articles and essays, researched and written before that book, in which critical elements of the creativity thesis were initially discovered, developed, and advanced. This book thus provides a crucial conceptual bridge between, on the one hand, my earlier research on technological innovation and regional development and, on the other hand, my more recent concern for creativity, diversity, and economic growth.

I have long been a student of the former, concerned for almost my entire career with how technological advancements help regions, urban centers, and nations to grow. I came late in my career to issues having to do with arts, culture, and diversity. When I address audiences interested primarily in these topics, I always start with an apology: "I am not a student of any of the three," I say, "and I have only a cursory understanding of their internal functionings. Rather, my career-long concern has been with how and why regions or nations grow economically." This compilation of essays should help to illustrate the overall trajectory of my work, from my ongoing interest in the nature of capitalism and the forces that power its growth to my ever-evolving understanding of the role that regions and urban centers play as the key economic and social organizing units of contemporary societies.

It has been more than two years now since *The Rise of the Creative Class* was published. In that time, its arguments have become the focus of considerable debate. Some of this debate has taken place within academia, blossoming in the fields of economics, geography, regional studies, urban planning, sociology, applied management, and the social sciences. But the debate has also stretched to journalism, public policy, and a huge number of professional communities, from urban development to arts and culture. Now it has begun to spill over into larger national conversations, touching on everything from the nature of quality economic development to the role of diversity and gay rights in twenty-first century society. This has been exciting and gratifying, and I couldn't have asked for a more well-intentioned group of both critics and proponents.

But, as is so often the case in wide-ranging dialogues, a good deal of the popular debate over these ideas has become diluted, ill informed, or overly ideological. In such exchanges, core ideas can get muddled or misused, and straw-man arguments can begin to overwhelm honest and forthright discussion. What I'd like to do here, then, is to clarify the key elements of the creativity theory, and to inject it into the larger context of ongoing intellectual and public discourse.

This chapter is divided into four main sections. To begin, I'll take some time to reprise my core theory on creativity and cities. Then, I'll take a step back to explain where my ideas come from; for, although they clearly reflect larger intellectual arcs and contributions, they are also deeply personal in nature, growing out of critical events and circumstances in my life. Next—and in the context of broader questions regarding technology, culture, and economic development—I'll outline what I believe to be the central issues in the ongoing debate over *The Rise of the Creative Class*. I'll conclude by summarizing the key issues that have emerged in this debate and in the evolution of my own thinking.

Creativity and Cities, Revisited

There can be little doubt that the age we are living through is one of tremendous economic and social transformation. Roughly a century ago, our economy and society changed from an agricultural to an industrial system. The change we are undergoing today is at least as large as that one, and brings with it sweeping implications for the way we work and live, the way we organize our time, the nature of family and community structures, and the role and function of urban centers.

Despite the massive migration to the cities and away from agricultural labor, even as late as 1950 less than 15 percent of the U.S. population could have been characterized as creative workers. Over the past two decades, though, creativity has become the driving force of our economy, and the creative sector has exploded, adding more than 20 million jobs. Globally, a third of the workers in advanced industrial nations are employed in the creative sector, engaged in science and engineering, research and development, and the technology-based industries, in arts, music, culture, and aesthetic and design work, or in the knowledge-based professions of health care, finance, and law. This creative sector accounts for nearly half of all wage and salary income in the United States—as much as the manufacturing and service sectors combined (see Table 1.1).

I should interject here that perhaps the single most overlooked—and single most important—element of my theory is the idea that *every*

Table 1.1 The Creative Economy

SECTOR	NUMBER OF WORKERS	SHARE	WAGES (BILLIONS)	SHARE	AVERAGE SALARY
Creative Sector	38,893,360	30.1%	$1,993	47.0%	$51,244
Manufacturing Sector	33,498,670	26.0%	$966	22.8%	$28,852
Service Sector	56,171,370	43.5%	$1,273	30.0%	$22,657
Total	129,024,100		$4,241		$32,869

Source: Compiled by Kevin Stolarick from Bureau of Labor Statistics data.

human being is creative. Some have criticized my work by saying that the very idea of a "Creative Class" is elitist and exclusionary. In my view, it is neither. In fact, I came to use this term out of a personal and intellectual frustration with the snobbery of concepts such as *knowledge workers, information society, high-tech economy,* and the like. I chose the term because I found it to be both more accurate in defining the real source of economic value-creation—that is, human creativity—and because it is an intellectual construct that extends to all forms of human potential: the vast storehouse and virtually limitless resource that is human creative capacity.

Tapping and stoking the creative furnace inside every human being is the great challenge of our time. Finding mechanisms and strategies to make this happen is the key to greater productivity, improved working and living conditions, and more sustainable patterns of development. "Creative Class" is the shorthand I use to describe the roughly one-third of U.S. and global workers who have the good fortune to be compensated monetarily for their creative output. But, make no mistake, creativity is as biologically and intellectually innate a characteristic to *all* human beings as thought itself.

For me, the most disturbing fact remains that *only* one-third of the workforce is employed in the creative sector of the economy. That means two-thirds are not. I had a hunch while writing *The Rise of the Creative Class* that inequality in our society was being exacerbated by the rise of the creative economy. My Carnegie Mellon collaborator Kevin Stolarick and I developed an Inequality Index that compares the wages of creative sector workers to those in the manufacturing sectors. We found that inequality is actually highest in the creative epicenters of the U.S. economy—places like San Francisco, the North Carolina Research Triangle, Washington, D.C., and Austin, Texas.

Ironically, creativity is the great leveler. It cannot be handed down, and it cannot be owned in the traditional sense. It defies gender, race, ethnicity, sexual orientation, and outward appearance. We cannot know in advance who the next Andy Warhol, Billie Holiday, Paul Allen, or Jimi Hendrix will be, or where he or she will come from. Yet our society continues to encourage the inventive talents of a minority while neglecting the creative capacities of the majority. We must be more imaginative in finding ways to make service, and even manufacturing, jobs more creative and thus less deadening for the people who hold them.

Much of the controversy over *The Rise of the Creative Class* stems from my arguments concerning the broad relationship between culture and economic growth. Social and economic theorists from Max Weber to Edward Banfield and Daniel Bell have argued that culture affects economic growth by producing incentives (as with Weber's "Protestant Work Ethic") that promote effort, thrift, and hard work. Culture, according to this view, motivates economic growth by focusing human energy and effort on work, and away from the pull of distractions such as leisure, play, sexuality, and other forms of non-work-related enjoyment. Left to their own devices, lacking firm rules, and without strong social and economic incentives, humans tend to defer work for other forms of enjoyment. Bell went so far as to identify culture as the core contradiction of modern capitalism, seeing the rise of a more open, expressive, and hedonistic culture during the 1960s as undermining the effort, incentives, and discipline that power innovation, entrepreneurship, and economic growth.

The creativity thesis breaks with these traditional conceptions in a few important ways. It argues that the role of culture is much more expansive, that human beings have limitless potential, and that the key to economic growth is to enable and unleash that potential. This unleashing requires an open culture—one that does not discriminate, does not force people into boxes, allows us to be ourselves, and validates various forms of family and of human identity. In this sense, culture operates not by constraining the range of human creative possibilities but by facilitating and mobilizing them. By extension, open culture on the macro level is a spur to societal innovation, entrepreneurship, and economic development.

My view of creativity and cities revolves around a simple formula, the 3 T's of economic growth: technology, talent, and tolerance. Economists have long argued that technology is the key to economic growth. MIT's Robert Solow won a Nobel Prize for his work in isolating technology as the driving force in economic growth. Stanford University economist Paul Romer argues that growth is an endogenous process, based on the continuous accumulation and exploitation of human knowledge. I agree wholeheartedly that technology plays a fundamental role in economic growth. In fact, I consider it so important that I made it my first T.

Talent is the second variable in my model. Other leading academics in the field, including the Nobel Prize winner Robert Lucas, have argued that growth is a consequence of *human capital*, a view shared by urban economist Edward Glaesar of Harvard University. In this view, the role of cities is to bring together and augment human capital, and places with more human capital grow more rapidly than those with less. Lucas refers to cities' human capital augmenting functions as "Jane Jacobs' externalities," and has suggested that she deserves a Nobel Prize for that idea. In this sense, urbanization is a key element of innovation and productivity growth.

I agree with this general principle, too. For talent, though, I substitute a measure of creative occupations for the typical education-based measure of human capital. The two are highly correlated, of course, but measuring *creative capital* (which is to say, creative occupations) includes people based on their current work rather than merely their education levels. In independent tests, Robert Cushing of the University of Texas at Austin has found that this creative capital measure performed better than the less specific human capital at predicting innovation and growth. This measure of creative occupations has the added advantage of being a better tool (than simply counting the number of people with college degrees) for allowing nations and regions to assess and capitalize upon their particular creative capital assets.

The third T, tolerance, is the key factor in enabling places to mobilize and attract technology and talent. Although economists have always recognized some form of technology or talent as important drivers of economic growth, we tend to think of them in the same way we think of the more conventional factors of production, such as raw materials—that is, as constituting a stock. According to this view, a place is endowed with certain stocks of technology and talent, both of which account for its rates of innovation and growth. But resources like technology, knowledge, and human capital differ in a fundamental way from the more traditional factors of production like land or raw materials; they are not fixed stocks, but transient *flows*. Technology and talent are highly mobile factors, flowing into and out of places.

Which brings us to the question: What accounts for the ability of some places to secure a greater quantity or quality of these flows? The answer, according to the creativity theory, lies in openness, diversity, and tolerance. Our work finds a strong connection between successful technology- and talent-harnessing places and places that are open to immigrants, artists, gays, and racial integration. These are the kinds of places that, by allowing people to be themselves and to validate their distinct identities, mobilize and attract the creative energy that bubbles up naturally from all walks of life. Such places gain an economic advantage in both harnessing the creative capabilities of a broader range of their own people and in capturing a disproportionate share of the flow.

Our work with Meric Gertler and Tara Vinodrai, for instance, found a direct correlation between diversity and high-tech growth in an analysis of Canadian regions. The research group National Economics has found a similar relationship in their independent analysis of Australian regions. And empirical research by the economists Gianmarco Ottaviano of the University of Bologna and Giovanni Peri of the University of California at Davis also corroborates this view, providing further independent confirmation of the effect of diversity and openness on economic growth for a large sample of U.S. city regions.

Where My Ideas Come From

The notion that cities spur human creativity is an old one, and the social and economic trends that my theory seeks to describe have been centuries in the making. The creativity theory does not pretend to exist outside the realm of history, nor would it be very useful if it did. It is instead a continuation of a larger body of work, one that goes far beyond my own humble reach. For my part, I have been developing these ideas in my work for more than two decades now. During that time, I have had the good fortune to learn from great thinkers and to build upon the classics of economic, social, and political theory. I have had the opportunity to collaborate with many incredibly talented people, to discuss and debate my ideas widely, and to work with numerous professionals on real world problems and strategies.

But my interest in creativity and economic development goes far beyond intellectual curiosity and is intimately tied to my personal history. At the risk of being a little self-indulgent, it might be helpful if I told you a bit about where this work and its author both come from.

I was born in the late 1950s in Newark, New Jersey. The Newark of my childhood memories was a lively, ethnically diverse, and thriving city. Nearly my entire extended family lived there: my grandparents and seven sets of aunts, uncles, and cousins, on both my mother's and my father's sides. I vividly recall Sunday afternoons at my maternal grandmother's house on North 6th Street, where I was surrounded by scores of extended family members and friends. But, most of all, I remember the feel of the larger community, the network of dense social capital that I would later come to appreciate intellectually through the work of Robert Putnam and others. In my mind's eye, I can still picture the Newark of that time. It was the energetic and vibrant place about which Phillip Roth writes, filled with shops and large department stores, incredible museums and libraries, a mosaic of ethnic neighborhoods, and the incredible industrial complex of the iron-bound or *down-neck* section of the city, where thousands of blue-collar workers made their livings.

During the 1960s, I saw it all go south. The bustling city of my youth fell into a vicious cycle of decline. As a child of that tumultuous decade, the civil rights movement and the race riots of 1967 had an indelible impact on me. For someone of my age, and certainly for me, these issues had an even greater impact than the Vietnam War. The Newark of those later days was an altogether different place: the once-animated city torn apart, tanks stationed at intersections, soldiers occupying volatile streets and neighborhoods. I remember driving down one of

Newark's grand avenues one evening, on the way home with my father from my weekly guitar lesson. We were waved over by armed guardsmen who nervously informed us that "snipers were shooting" in an adjacent building.

The stark reality of racial tension and the deteriorating urban condition had a haunting effect on me, though of course I couldn't have grasped it fully at the time. Why was Newark exploding into violence? What could be motivating such conflict? These gut reactions would eventually morph into more sophisticated formulations: What in our economy and society could produce such undeniable racial and class inequality? At the time, though, the feelings were personal and visceral.

I was further shaped by the world of my father's factory, as I talk about in *The Rise of the Creative Class*. My father was employed by Victory Optical, in Newark's iron-bound section. He started work there in his teens and, after serving in World War II, returned to the factory, where he labored his way up the ladder from regular factory worker, to foreman, to one of the plant managers. I was always fascinated—as most young boys are—by the place where my father worked, and I wanted to know more about it. He would take me there sometimes on Saturdays, and I was drawn into this world. My father would tell me about the products Victory Optical made, about the machines that did the work, and—most importantly, he always stressed—about the men who provided the talent the factory needed to keep it running. In his eyes, it was their knowledge, intelligence, and creativity that made the plant special.

The factory, like so many other American factories, declined in the late 1960s and 1970s, finally shuttering its doors in the late 1970s. This event left its mark on me, clearly shaping my later fascinations with technological change, the nature of work on the factory floor, systems of production organization, and the spatial location and organization of industries.

Looking back on it, I realize now it was the intersection of these two intensely personal worlds—the wrenching urban conflicts of Newark and the heartbreaking decline of my father's factory—that foreshadowed my enduring personal interest in the intersection of economic transformation and place. Mirroring as they did the broader transformation of America's older urban centers and the deindustrialization of the American economy, these events spurred my youthful intellect. I wanted to know why these things were happening; what broader forces were setting them in motion? For obvious reasons, it was hard to get anything approaching a thorough answer from the adults who had to live through such highly charged situations. So, as a young boy, I turned my attention to the world of books.

On Saturdays, my father and I would drive first to the factory where he worked the morning shift, and then get a lunch of pizza and hotdogs in Newark's Italian district. After lunch, my father would take me to the Newark Public Library, where I spent countless hours as a young teenager roaming those magnificent stacks, searching through all sorts of books in the urban affairs section. There, I was introduced to the thinking of some of the greatest urbanists, social scientists, and public intellectuals of the day: Daniel Bell, Jane Jacobs, Daniel Patrick Moynihan, Nathan Glaser, Edward Banfield, Michael Harrington, John Kenneth Galbraith, and countless others. Delving deeply into this world of ideas and social commentary, I pored over pages and pages on the city, on ethnicity and race, and on urban affairs and federal programs.

My high school years, during the early 1970s, drove me even more intensely to the study of these issues. Like many Italian-Americans of my generation, I attended Catholic high school—Queen of Peace Boys High School in North Arlington, New Jersey. There, I had the good fortune to encounter several superb educators. Some were members of the Christian Brothers but many were secular teachers, or what we referred to as "lay" teachers, who broadened my interest and stoked my intellect. The ones who had the most influence on me were younger teachers, recent graduates from New Jersey colleges and from the University of Pennsylvania. Caught up as they were in the events of the day, their courses fueled my passion for urban issues. Armed with endless resources from the Newark Public Library, I began writing term papers on the nature of cities, housing and urban affairs, the location of manufacturing, and so on.

In 1975, I received a Garden State scholarship, which enabled me to "go away" to college at Rutgers University, some 30 miles down the turnpike in New Brunswick, New Jersey. College was the turning point for me; I was able at Rutgers to refine my thinking and home in on the intersection of economic transformation and place that had interested me for so long. I dug into political science, economics, geography, sociology, and ultimately urban affairs and urban planning. Rutgers, at the time, was an amazing place, filled with the energy of the 1960s and boasting incredible professors in the social sciences, and especially in urban planning. I took courses with remarkable faculty: Robert Beauregard and Susan Fainstein in the planning program, Robert Lake in geography, and Stephen Bronner in political science. And, for the first time, I found a group of peers who also had an interest in intellectual pursuits. After class, friends and I would retire to the local bars and pubs where we discussed economic, social, and political issues late into the night.

I discovered something about my interests in those formative years: They were both intellectual and pragmatic. I was interested in the abstract, to be certain, and took courses in social theory. I read classical political theory, the Frankfurt School, and critical theory, Lukacs, Gramsci, Adorno, and Horkeimer, the theory of the State, O'Connor, Habermas, Miliband, Poulantzas, and others, and urban affairs running the gamut from Banfield, Moynihan, and Glaser, to Paul Davidoff, Alan Altshuler, and Jane Jacobs, to David Harvey, Manuel Castells, Bennett Harrison, and more.

But I also found myself drawn to the real world problems of actual cities and communities. I took a job at the Center for Urban Policy, working for Robert Lake on a large-scale research project exploring "Black suburbs." I wrote on the fiscal stress experienced by my hometown, conducting field research and interviews with key subjects. I undertook an honors thesis on housing policy and the State, shaped by the then-raging debate over the nature of the State in capitalist economies.

A second crucial turning point occurred during my graduate school years. I went to study political science and urban planning at MIT and later took a PhD in Urban Planning at Columbia University. My sojourn to MIT included truly memorable seminars with Bennett Harrison on urban political economy, labor market theory, and deindustrialization. This was at the time when Michael Piore and Charles Sabel were conducting the research for their landmark book, *The Second*

Industrial Divide, on the tensions between hierarchical and flexible models of economic organization. I worked with Alan Altshuler on urban affairs and with Thomas Ferguson on political economy. I continued to work on the nature of the State and wrote a paper on the subject that I presented at a Harvard University conference in honor of the late Talcott Parsons.

At Columbia, I delved into housing and urban issues and took courses with Peter Marcuse, Neil Smith, Elliott Sclar, Harvey Goldstein, and Mark Kesselman. I gazed ever more deeply into theories of political economy, economic transformation, place, and the city, meanwhile deepening my historical understanding by reading the urban history associated with Sam Bass Warner, Roy Lubove, Sam Hays, and Joel Tarr, the labor history of David Montgomery and others, and all variants of economic and business history, from Charles Beard to Alfred Chandler. I developed a keen interest in the labor process through the work of Harry Bravereman and Richard Edwards. I became intrigued by the process of technological innovation *a la* the extraordinary work of Christopher Freeman, Richard Nelson, and Sidney Winter, by Daniel Bell and others on post-industrial society, by Peter Drucker on the nature of knowledge work, and by Jane Jacobs on the nature of cities.

Around this time, I came across the emerging theory of economic transformation as laid out by the European regulation school of political economy, associated with Michel Aglietta, Alain Lipietz, and others who sought a grand synthesis of Marx, Schumpeter, and Keynes. At the risk of gross oversimplification, this body of work argued that capitalism was undergoing an epochal turn from what was termed a Fordist economic system to a post-Fordist one. The Fordist system was based on the advances of Frederick Taylor and Henry Ford in building new assembly line frameworks of mass production that realized incredible output efficiencies by breaking tasks down into their elemental components. It used the technique of scientific management to allocate tasks and organize the division of labor, combining these divisions with the moving assembly line in order to control and accelerate the pace of work.

The regulation school went one critical step further. It argued that what made the Fordist system work was a complimentary system for organizing demand based on mass consumption. The success of the Fordist system was therefore also predicated upon the synthesis, or balancing, of production and consumption. Mass consumption had, as its premise, a whole series of policies and social innovations, many of which had a huge impact on the structure of urban areas. Unionization, made possible by the Wagner Act, enabled workers' wages to rise, and then set in motion a system of wage increases tied to productivity increase. Suburbanization fueled mass consumption. And this suburbanization was based on federal initiatives in housing finance, which ushered in new (at the time) long-term mortgages and the interstate highway system, allowing for still more suburban development. These innovations and approaches created the wage base and the effective demand—mass consumption—that was required to stimulate and reproduce the mass production economy.

This system, these authors argued, began to break down in the 1970s and 1980s. The question was raised: What kind of system would replace it? The open answer of what might come after Fordism was captured in the then-popular construct of *post-Fordism*. In their provocative and influential work, Piore and Sabel argued that what would supplant the system of mass production Fordism was a more specialized and flexible system based on networks of small- to medium-sized firms. Their work reverberated through the fields of geography and urban studies, motivating the research and writings of Annalee Saxenian, Allen Scott, Michael Storper, Ann Marksuen, Amy Glasmeir, Meric Gertler, Phil Cooke, and Kevin Morgan, among others. Later and more indirectly it even motivated the Harvard Business School's Michael Porter, with his focus on the importance of geographically concentrated networks of firms, or *clusters*, as a new model of economic organization.

The third, and perhaps most critical, turning point in my intellectual journey occurred when I was a faculty member at Ohio State University in the mid-1980s. In 1984, I took my first academic job in the Department of City and Regional Planning, and within my first month there something happened that truly changed my life. Into my office one day bounded an energetic and immensely curious colleague named Martin Kenney. It was immediately obvious that here was a person specially endowed not only with a facile intellect and a solid grasp of cutting edge theory, but also with an uncanny knack for understanding the very real and very material evolution of capitalism. Kenney had just completed a dissertation at Cornell on the biotechnology industry, and had also conducted several studies of Japanese high-tech industry. Piore's and Sabel's *The Second Industrial Divide* had just come out, and debate was brewing over its characterization of flexible industrial districts as a new model of economic organization.

Kenney and I were keen on this debate, and on defining for ourselves the nature and trajectory of post-Fordist capitalism. We put together a study group of graduate students from across the university and met nearly daily to discuss the issue. But how would we combine our apparently unrelated interests, mine in regional development and Kenney's in high-tech industries? One day, it came to us: venture capital. This was a key aspect of the emerging system of high-technology capitalism, and yet it was virtually unexamined outside of mainly descriptive studies.

We went to work immediately, conducting field research and interviews with dozens of venture capitalists in Silicon Valley and the Route 128 area around Boston. We did archival research at the Harvard Business School library and in Silicon Valley, and built a large database from these sources on venture capital investments, flows, and networks of co-investment. We developed the construct that high-tech innovation took place in regionally defined *social structures of innovation*, in which locally embedded venture capitalists played a critical gate-keeping role by identifying and monitoring investments and attracting outside sources of capital.

It turned out that the project brought together many strands of my former lives: my interest in the intersection of economic transformation and place, in theories of economic transformation and social structure, and in the ways in which the theoretical and the practical intertwine. But something else struck us. The venture capital model was not a full-blown model of economic organization on the order of Fordism. Certainly it was technologically innovative, but it did not, we argued, have the broad systemic power of Fordism that would allow it to give rise to, and to reproduce, a new universal structure linking production and consumption. It was, we concluded, an early and incomplete response to the emerging post-Fordist age.

So we began to look into other systems of economic organization with which to compare the U.S. high-technology model. Several global models came to mind: the flexibly specialized and deeply embedded industrial districts that Piore and Sable had identified in the Third Italy, the German system of high-value-added manufacturing, and, finally, what we began to see as the emerging system of post-Fordist Japanese production. Kenney had already been exploring, and had even begun writing about, the Japanese system. We dug into the literature on Japan's political economy, from Ruth Benedict to Robert Cole and James Abegglen. We saw in this system a new and more advanced model for harnessing the intellectual and creative energy of workers: a system of production that channeled workers' natural energy through the use of *kaizen* techniques, suggestion systems, worker involvement in quality circles, team-based work, rotation, and supplier involvement.

Around this time, Honda opened a plant—the first major Japanese automotive plant on American soil—in Marysville, Ohio, a suburb of Columbus near Ohio State University. Equipped at first only with our interest in Japanese economic organization, we immediately launched a small research project, collecting background data and visiting the Marysville plant. Simply put, we were blown away. We quickly geared up for a major research effort on the Japanese system and its transfer abroad to America.

Kenney and I argued that the Japanese system represented an advance over Fordism in that it more fully tapped the intrinsic capabilities of shop-floor workers through the aforementioned methods of workplace interaction. We built a huge data set of hundreds of firms, detailed the location of the firms and their characteristics, and then, with the support of the Sloan Foundation, conducted a sizeable mail survey of their operations. Our analyses revealed that these companies were in fact transferring core elements of their new production system to the United States, and that these elements were working well with American workers in the U.S. environment. The system was generating considerable performance and productivity benefits. This, to us, seemed a much more universally applicable economic response to the post-Fordist era than the U.S. high-tech model.

Kenney and I ultimately wrote two books addressing the natures of both of these transformative economic approaches and their spatial implications. In *The Breakthrough Illusion* (Basic Books, 1990), we out-lined the U.S. mode of high-tech innovation premised upon venture capital and entrepreneurial startup companies and organized in geo-graphically concentrated networks such as Silicon Valley. The book delved into the limits and tensions of this model, for it was our belief that it was a partial and somewhat elitist response to the times. We dealt with the hyper-mobility of high-tech labor, the downsides of the high-tech age, and the problems of failing to integrate larger segments of the workforce or society into the overall picture.

Our second book, *Beyond Mass Production* (Oxford University Press, 1993), took up the Japanese response to post-Fordism in earnest. It asked the questions: Was the Japanese system a break with Fordism; did it hold within it the seeds of a new post-Fordist structure; and, if so, was that system transferable to outside of Japan? We analyzed the mechanisms that Japanese companies used to harness the knowledge and intelligence of factory workers, exploring the characteristics of this model in sectors from automobiles to electronics. We examined the cross-national transfer and adaptation of the Japanese model to the United States in the automotive, rubber and tire, steel, and electronics industries. Finally, we considered the model's downsides: its limits as a full-blown production system, the way it continued to exploit workers, and its dependence upon a highly structured system to bind workers' energies to companies.

In the late 1980s, I moved to Carnegie Mellon University. Kenney and I continued our work on post-Fordist economic models, publishing follow-up papers on U.S. high-tech and on Japan, including work on Japanese factories in Mexico. I began to look for evidence of the trans-mission of these new production and work organization systems into U.S. companies, conducting a study of the diffusion of such practices, which I referred to as "high-performance work systems," to indigenous manufacturing companies in the American Midwest.

I extended this work on high-performance manufacturing to con-sider several advanced environmental manufacturing practices. With funding from the National Science Foundation, I embarked on a study of the relationship between new systems of production organization and pollution prevention. I wanted to examine how new models of high-performance or post-Fordist production affected pollution, environmental outputs, and sustainable development. The project concluded that companies were not pursuing environmental programs for environmental ends *per se*, but that they were doing so as part of their broader attempts to implement high-performance manufacturing. Later, again with the support of the Sloan Foundation, I undertook a massive field research project on the globalization of the automotive industry, working closely with a former University of California-Berkeley graduate student and superb field researcher, Timothy Sturgeon.

Perhaps it was the influence of Carnegie Mellon's distinct academic-industrial atmosphere, but over time my work began to shift back toward the study of technical innovation. I undertook a large survey project with Wesley Cohen and W. Richard Goe (a former Ohio State graduate student) on university-industry research centers. We documented the extent of these centers and surveyed their internal operations. Working with the historian David Hounhsell and a young doctoral student named Mark Samber, we delved into the history of university–industry relationships, and I was quickly convinced that the university had developed a model of organization that not only motivated its scientists, but that also had a huge impact on early research laboratories.

Wrapped up in these issues, I embarked on a sabbatical leave in the mid-1990s to the Center for Science, Technology, and Public Policy at Harvard University. There, I worked with Lewis Branscomb, Fumio Kodama, Harvey Brooks, and others on a major study of U.S. and Japanese innovation systems, and the role of the university within them. I began to study the research and development (R&D) process in more detail, and conducted an extensive study of foreign or transplant R&D labs in the U.S. We built a massive database of the location, establishment, and growth of these labs, conducted field visits and interviews with them, and ultimately carried out a large-scale survey of all of the labs.

At this time, another critical turning point occurred in my thinking on the role of creative people (whom I later came to term "talent") in the innovation process. The R&D lab study brought us to the important finding that, unlike manufacturing transplants, foreign labs were not seeking to transfer their indigenous management system to the

United States, but rather were emulating the kind of organizational structures found in U.S. research labs and universities. There was something about the open, peer-oriented environment of the university that was extremely successful in motivating scientists and what we then called "knowledge workers." These labs allowed their scientists to publish, they held seminars, and they invited visiting scientists from universities and other labs to make presentations, and at times to work there. They were in effect adapting their organization to meet the intellectual needs of these knowledge workers. Or, to use the organizational theorist Karl Weick's phrase, these knowledge workers were "enacting" the environments they required to work effectively.

The role of talent in the R&D process was driven home to me rather innocuously one day, as I was interviewing the former director of R&D for a leading Japanese electronics company. When I asked him why his company had started a major high-end U.S. lab, his answer prompted me to reconsider the role of these facilities as what I would later call "talent magnets." He said that the opening of a major high-end R&D facility in the United States did much more than simply add research capability; it functioned as a "talent attractor," allowing his company to recruit higher quality scientists and engineers for its faculties around the world. I began at that moment to think of innovation not merely as a process of technological invention, but also as a process of organizing and mobilizing talent.

My next step was to insert the issue of talent into the study of regional development. For years, I had observed the attempts made by Pittsburgh (where I then lived) and other older industrial cites to revitalize their economies by stimulating the development of high-tech industries. These regions had invested heavily in various combinations of technology transfer and commercialization, university-industry partnerships, entrepreneurial incubation, and venture capital. Time and again, though, these programs appeared to make little or no difference. The regions continued to generate inventions, even startup companies, and also to cultivate a great deal of highly educated technical talent—but virtually all of that talent leaked away to other regions.

At this time, my Carnegie Mellon colleague Wesley Cohen had been developing his pioneering concept of *absorptive capacity* to explain how successful firms undertook technological innovation not only to generate new ideas and inventions, but to improve their ability to absorb knowledge from outside. I immediately made the connection to the regional scene. What distinguished some innovative high-tech regions from others, including Pittsburgh, was their ability not just to generate innovations, but to go one necessary step further in absorbing them. And for this (as Chapters 2, 3, and especially 7 explain) they needed a broadly supportive community context that could attract and retain talent in addition to generating it.

Upon returning to Carnegie Mellon, I picked up this agenda in earnest, spurred in part by the continued movement of talented people and new startup firms (such as Lycos) out of Pittsburgh. For decades, my entire academic field had focused its energies on charting, following, and predicting the location of firms and industries. The question I decided to ask was different: What motivates the location decisions of *people*? And to go with that common sense question: how do *peoples'* location decisions affect the ability of places to innovate and spur economic growth?

I looked for ways to begin to get a handle on these deceptively simple queries. First, I launched a project on sustainable development, examining how environmental assets factored into the location decisions of firms and people. This eventually turned into a study of talent via focus groups and interviews, and then statistical research (see Chapters 3 and 4). I began with crude measures of both knowledge workers (whom I would later come to redefine as the *creative class*) and of quality of place, which we measured by using various indicators of so-called amenities. Unsatisfied with these initial measures, my team and I began to focus on the development of more systematic and reliable indicators of the *revealed location preferences* of various groups.

We developed the Bohemian Index (see Chapter 5)—a measure of the concentration of working artists, musicians, and the like in a given area—in order to examine what effect such concentrations had on the location of both high creative capital individuals and high-technology firms and industries. Working with Gary Gates, currently of the Urban Institute, we used the Gay Index to probe the relationship between diversity, creative capital, and high-tech industry growth (see Chapter 6). With a fantastic team of graduate students and colleagues including Gates, Stolarick, Sam Youl Lee, Brian Knudsen, Irene Tinagli, and others, we conducted the analyses that make up the chapters of this book.

The Great Creative Class Debate

With these issues swirling in my head, I wrote *The Rise of the Creative Class* from 1999 to 2001, mainly in the summers of 2000 and 2001. The book went through several iterations and many titles. My main objective was not to write about high-technology industry or the so-called new economy, but to track the more fundamental and enduring economic—and especially social and cultural—forces at work in American society. The book has been successful beyond my wildest dreams, and has generated intense debate and controversy, by which I am both intrigued and humbled.

Perhaps not surprisingly, given the political tenor of our times, it has been the cultural aspects of my work—particularly my ideas regarding the relationship between demographic diversity, innovation, and economic growth—that have generated much of the controversy. Indeed, the intensity of my critics on this score has surprised me. Consider this: In the period since *The Rise of the Creative Class* was published, I have been accused of eroding traditional family values (I don't), of promoting a gay agenda (I'm straight), and of undermining the very tenets of Judeo-Christian civilization (I'm at a loss).

Comments like these make it clear to me that there are more than academic issues at stake here. In the Foreword to the Australian edition of *The Rise of the Creative Class*, management consultant Terry Cutler sums it up well. Cutler recounts a meeting of distinguished intellectuals and civic leaders to whom he presented my key ideas concerning diversity and economic growth. "Summoning up my courage," he writes, "I described Florida's findings about the correlation between bohemianism and diversity in the location of high-tech firms. The palpable recoil around the room at such a radical and distasteful recipe for success left me in no doubt that these civic leaders would clearly prefer to drift into a genteel poverty." This need to hold on to a conventional social order, even if it means forfeiting economic growth and the well being of societies as a whole, is what I see as the principal barrier to the fuller development of the emerging creative economy.

Jane Jacobs has a word to describe this kind of behavior. She calls it "squelching." Jacobs believes that all cities have creative energy and that all people are creative. What distinguishes thriving cities from struggling cities is a group of people she dubs "squelchers." Squelchers, Jacobs explains, are those political, business, and civic leaders who divert and derail human creative energy by posing roadblocks, acting as gatekeepers, and saying "no" to new ideas, regardless of their merit. What worries me is that, even when they are wrong on the facts, my critics have continued to provide ample ammunition for such squelchers.

The harsh and personal nature of some of these attacks initially took me by surprise. As an academic and social scientist, though, I try always to keep in mind that debate is a healthy thing. It enables—indeed, forces—us to clarify and refine our ideas, to move toward newer and more comprehensive understandings based on verifiable facts as opposed to opinions, and to take our critics' valid points into consideration.

One line of criticism of the creativity theory claims that I misread the causes of economic growth. The argument here is that regional growth comes from a combination of low costs, traditional business recruitment attraction, and family values, rather than open environments geared to "singles, young people, homosexuals, sophistos, and trendoids." The implication is that this is a zero-sum game—that a region can be either family friendly or gay and bohemian friendly, but not both. Politically, this is divisive thinking; worse, it's economically inaccurate. Many popular lists of America's most family- or child-friendly cities turn out to be loaded with cities that also score high as homes for gays and artists. As *The Rise of the Creative Class* demonstrated, the top five child-friendly major metros in the United States are Portland, Oregon; Seattle, Washington; Minneapolis, Minnesota; New York City, and San Francisco. All but one of these five ranked well above average on the Gay Index, and all five were in the top seven on our Bohemian Index.

The most successful regions welcome all kinds of people. They offer a range of living choices, from nice suburbs with single-family housing to hip urban districts for the unattached. Why do they offer all of the above? Simple: because they have to. Like it or not, only 23.5 percent of Americans now live in a standard nuclear family with two parents and children at home. More young people are delaying marriage and child-birth. More adults than ever before are separating or divorcing. Many of us live in some sort of alternative personal arrangement. Appealing only to traditional families and bashing everyone else may make good propaganda for the culture wars, but as a development strategy, it's a pretty narrow approach. And any region or politician that clings to this increasingly obsolete *my way or the highway* attitude stands to alienate a lot of talented people.

A number of critics, in response to this diversity argument, have brought up the example of Silicon Valley: "isn't it a staid, boring place," they say, "that appeals mainly to conventional engineering types?" I have argued that Silicon Valley can only be understood in relation to the adventurous culture and innovative research universities of the entire Bay Area—a place where early hippie entrepreneurs like Jobs and Wozniak were not merely accepted, but actually financed by venture capitalists. Today, gays and urban singles commute from San Francisco to work in Silicon Valley, while family-oriented professionals live in Silicon Valley suburbs and work in downtown San Francisco. What gives the Bay Area its advantage is that it has something for everyone.

My work has also been criticized from the left. Here, I am painted as a vapid elitist and a starry-eyed huckster for creativity and flexibility, still promoting the New Economy although failing to see how the real econ-omy exploits the masses. That strikes me as strange, to say the least. In fact, *The Rise of the Creative Class* takes aim at the 1990s New Economy fantasies and has little to do with making cities yuppie friendly, though leftist critics have tried to frame it (and therefore belittle its arguments) in that way. Rather, my core message is (I've said it before, and I'll say it again): human creativity is the ultimate source of economic growth. Every single person is creative in some way, and to fully tap and harness that creativity we must be tolerant, diverse, and inclusive. (This message is having real impact, too. To cite just one case: In Cincinnati, Procter & Gamble has joined with civic and gay activists in an attempt to overturn the heinous Article 12, which forbids the city from passing antidiscrimination legislation that would apply to gays and lesbians.)

Anyone who has read *The Rise of the Creative Class* will confirm that I clearly and thoroughly decried "the naïve optimism of the so-called New Economy," noting from the very first chapter that "not all is rosy" for workers today. "With no big company to provide security, we bear much more risk," I wrote, "suffering high levels of mental and emotional stress . . . We crave flexibility but have less time . . . The technologies that were supposed to liberate us have invaded our lives." Later I remind readers that, "flexibility does not mean the end of long hours . . . in fact, the long trajectory of modern capitalism has involved the relentless extension of the working day across time and space." A chapter called "The Time Warp" describes the many "insidious factors" that lead to overwork and stress. These critics prefer not to acknowledge that I have already made their arguments for them: "the real losers, in terms of overwork, are those holding two full-time minimum-wage jobs to support a family . . . [They] are a modern-day equivalent of the nineteenth century's burned-out factory laborers." If it isn't clear already, I am no unquestioning propagandist for the so-called New Economy and the Internet age.

Some critics go on to dismiss the advantage of places like San Francisco, Boston, Seattle, and Austin as mere flash-in-the-pan products of the 1990s dot-com bubble. But these places have been experiencing *quality* growth for decades, building solid new industries that have helped to strengthen our economy and change the world. Much has been made of the fact that 1990s growth centers like San Francisco, Seattle, and New York City are losing population. It's true that people are moving out of these and other places. But the simple fact that some people are leaving misses a much bigger point. Using IRS data to compare who's moving out to who's moving in, Robert Cushing of the University of Texas found that these regions are losing low-income but *gaining* high-income workers. These cities thus continue to gain competitive advantage, even as they lose raw numbers of people, further bolstering my arguments about what types of city characteristics spark quality economic growth.

A number of critics have tried to pick apart the creativity thesis by comparing the job-generating capabilities of different groups of regions. "Jobs data going back 20 years, to 1983," writes one right-wing critic, "show that Florida's top 10 cities, as a group, actually do worse, lagging behind the national economy by several percentage points, while his so-called least creative cities continue to look like economic powerhouses, expanding 60 percent faster than his most creative cities during that same period." Is this really true? To get a handle on the issue, my colleague Kevin Stolarick of Carnegie Mellon ran the job growth numbers for the period 1999 to 2002, the years since the initial Creativity Index was introduced. Stolarick found that higher job growth *was* actually associated with the regions that ranked higher on the Creativity Index.

As I have alluded to previously, though, looking only at the figures on overall job creation can be, by itself, extremely misleading. The creativity theory says that there are many types of growth. Indeed it argues that all growth is *not* created equal. My theory is concerned primarily with the *quality* of economic growth, and quality of growth is not reflected in job growth at all, but in the wages and incomes that people make. Stolarick's research found that wage growth between 1999 and 2002 was considerably better in regions ranking highly on the Creativity Index. Strikingly, these regions had higher wage growth in this period despite *already* boasting higher wages to begin with.

Las Vegas—a region typically held up as fast-growing by these critics, but which ranks low on my indicators—is a good example of what a *low*-quality growth center looks like. It's true that between 1990 and 2000, Las Vegas ranked first in population growth and third in job growth. But in *per capita* income growth, a measure of how much people make at their jobs, it was a miserable 294th out of the 315 U.S. Metropolitan Statistical Areas that existed in 1990.

Other detractors have suggested that my work falls victim to a classic chicken-and-egg problem. What typically comes first, they argue, are the jobs. Once a region has those, then the people—as well as the amenities, lifestyle, and tolerance—will follow. In theory, that's an insightful counterargument, but it's not exactly true. First of all, it is a well-known fact that increasing wealth for a city or region also means increasing gentrification. With gentrification comes an *out*-migration of bohemians (especially low-wage-end bohemians, the kind that a creative powerhouse like New York City boasts up and down every block). When I asked this what-comes-first question of Jane Jacobs, she wrly answered: "When a place gets boring, even the rich people leave."

Additionally, studies have shown that it does matter critically where people decide to locate. A 2002 survey of four thousand recent college graduates reported in the Wall Street Journal found that three-quarters of them identified location as more important than the availability of a job when selecting a place to live. In the graduates' thinking, it made more sense to pick several different locations in which to live first, and then to go back and find potential employers in those locations. This reminds us that real places are important. They provide the thick labor markets that help match people to jobs, mating markets that enable people to find life partners, social markets that encourage people to form meaningful friendships, and amenities that allow people to pursue the lifestyles they wish and the ability to validate their identities.

In the end, I welcome the opportunity to address my critics. It keeps me—and hopefully them, too—honest and open about our methods, findings, and conclusions. New ideas are always controversial, and they can always benefit from a thorough constructive critique. We desperately need more—not less—debate, discussion, and research on these subjects. Without further ado, I turn now to that research.

2

CITIES AND THE CREATIVE CLASS

"Great cities have always been melting pots of races and cultures. Out of the vivid and subtle interactions of which they have been the centers, there have come the newer breeds and the newer social types."
—*Robert Park*

From the seminal work of Alfred Marshall to the 1920 studies by Robert Park to the pioneering writings of Jane Jacobs, cities have captured the imagination of sociologists, economists, and urbanists. For Park, and especially for Jacobs, cities were cauldrons of diversity and difference, creativity and innovation. Yet over the last several decades, scholars have somehow forgotten the basic, underlying themes of urbanism. Generally speaking, the conventional wisdom about regional development for the past two decades has been that companies, firms, and industries drive regional innovation and growth, and thus there is an almost exclusive focus in the literature on the location, and more recently the clustering, of firms and industries. From a policy perspective, this basic conceptual approach has undergirded policies which seek to spur growth by offering firms financial inducements, incentives, and the like.

There have been some advances in recent times, however. Scholars such as Robert Putnam have focused on the social functions of neighborhoods, communities, and cities, while others, like Edward Glaesar and Terry Clark, have turned their attention toward human capital, consumption, and cities as lifestyle and entertainment districts. Only by moving forward from these new perspectives can we gain a better understanding of contemporary cities and communities. The intent of the overview of recent directions in urban studies that follows is just this— to spur wider commentary and debate on the critical functions of cities and regions in 21st century creative capitalism.

Why Geography Is Not Dead

Perhaps the greatest of all the modern myths about cities is that *geography is dead*. With the Internet and modern telecommunication and transportation systems, the thinking goes, it is no longer necessary for people who work together to *be* together, so they won't be. But this end of geography theme has been with us since the turn of the nineteenth century, when experts predicted than technologies from telegraph and the telephone to the automobile and the airplane would essentially kill off the cities. In his widely read 1998 book *New Rules for the New Economy,* Kevin Kelly wrote, "The New Economy operates in a *space* rather than a place, and over time more and more economic transactions will migrate to this new space."[1] Kelly then qualifies this to some degree, writing that: "Geography and real estate, however, will remain, well . . . real. Cities will flourish, and the value of a distinctive place, such as a wilderness area, or a charming hill village, will only increase. Still he reiterates that, "People will inhabit places, but increasingly the economy inhabits a space."

Never has a myth been easier to deflate. Not only do people remain highly concentrated, but the economy itself—the high-tech, knowledge-based, and creative content industries which drive so much of economic growth—continues to concentrate in specific places from Austin and Silicon Valley, to New York City and Hollywood, just as the automobile industry once concentrated in Detroit. Students of urban and regional growth, from Robert Park to Wilbur Thompson, have long pointed to the role of places as incubators of creativity, innovation, and new industries.[2] In addition, the death-of-place prognostications contradict the qualitative research I have conducted analyzing the role of place in an individual's location decisions. From the countless interviews, the focus groups I've observed, and the statistical research I've done, it is apparent that place and community are more critical factors than ever before. And it appears that place, rather than being an abstract *space* as Kelly suggests, is essential to economic life. The economy itself increasingly takes form around real concentrations of people in real places.

Many researchers, sociologists, and academics have theorized on the continued importance of place in economic and social life. An increasingly influential view suggests that place remains important as a locus of economic activity because of the tendency of firms to cluster together. This view builds on the influential theories of the economist Alfred Marshall, who argued that firms cluster in *agglomerations* to gain productive efficiencies. The contemporary variant of this view, advanced by Harvard Business School professor Michael Porter, has many proponents in academia and in the practice of economic development.[3] It is clear that similar firms tend to cluster. Examples of this sort of agglomeration include not only Detroit and Silicon Valley, but the *maquiladora* electronics-and-auto-parts districts in Mexico, the clustering of makers of disk drives in Singapore and of flat-panel displays in Japan, and the garment district and Broadway theater district in New York City.

The question is not whether firms cluster, but why. Several answers have been offered. Some experts believe that clustering captures efficiencies generated from tight linkages between firms. Others say it has to do with the positive benefits of co-location, or what they call *spillovers*. Still others claim it is because certain kinds of activity require face-to-face contact.[4] But these are only partial answers. More importantly, companies cluster in order to draw from concentrations of talented people who power innovation and economic growth. The ability to rapidly mobilize talent from such a concentration of people is a tremendous source of competitive advantage for companies in our time-driven and horizontal economy.

The Social Capital Perspective

An alternative view is based on Robert Putnam's social capital theory. From his perspective, regional economic growth is associated with tight-knit communities where people and firms form and share strong ties.[5] In his widely read book *Bowling Alone*, he makes a compelling argument that many aspects of community life declined precipitously over the last half of the twentieth century.[6] Putnam gets his title from his finding that from 1980 to 1993, league bowling declined by 40 percent, while the number of individual bowlers rose by 10 percent. This, he argues, is just one indicator of a broader and more disturbing trend. Across the nation, people are less inclined to be part of civic groups: Voter turnout is down, as is church attendance and union membership, and people are less and less inclined to volunteer. All of this stems from what Putnam sees as a long-term decline in social capital.

By this, he means that people have become increasingly disconnected from one another and from their communities. Putnam finds this disengagement in the declining participation in churches, political parties, and recreational leagues, not to mention the loosening of familial bonds. Through painstakingly detailed empirical research, he documents the decline in social capital in civic and social life.

For Putnam, declining social capital means that society becomes less trustful and less civic-minded. Putnam believes a healthy, civic-minded community is essential to prosperity. While initially Putnam's theory resonated with me, my own research indicates a wholly different trend. The people in my focus groups and interviews rarely wished for the kinds of community connectedness Putnam talks about. If anything, it appeared they were trying to get away from those kinds of environments. (Indeed, this has been a long-standing tradition among bohemians and creative types in America.[7]) While to a certain extent participants acknowledged the importance of community, they did not want it to be invasive, or to prevent them from pursuing their own lives. Rather, they desired what I have termed "quasi-anonymity." In the terms of modern sociology, these people prefer weak ties to strong.

This leads me to an even more basic observation. The kinds of communities both that we desire and that generate economic prosperity are different than those of the past. Social structures that were important in earlier years now work against prosperity. Traditional notions of what it means to be a close, cohesive community and society tend to inhibit economic growth and innovation. Where strong ties among people were once important, weak ties are now more effective. Those social structures that historically embraced exclusiveness and closeness may now appear restricting and invasive. These older communities are being exchanged for more inclusive and socially diverse arrangements. These trends are also what the statistics seem to bear out.

All of this raises deep questions that run to the very core of community and society. The life we think of as uniquely American—strong ties between families and friends, close neighborhoods, and the attributes that come along with such communities—civic clubs and vibrant electoral politics, to name a few, is giving way to communities with weaker ties, yet which are more inclusive. These newer communities are far more versed at generating economic growth and attracting high technology to a region. In the main, the ways that communities create economic growth has been transformed.

While historically exclusive, tightly connected communities were thought to be beneficial, though there are some theorists that argue the disadvantages of such tight bonds. Indeed, social capital can, and often does, cut both ways. While it can reinforce belonging and community, it can just as easily shut out newcomers, raise barriers to entry, and retard innovation. Adam Smith long ago noted this dilemma in his *Wealth of Nations*, lashing out at merchants who formed tightly knit cliques for precisely such reasons: "People of the same trade seldom meet together, even for merriment or diversion, but the conversation ends in a conspiracy against the public." Mancur Olson later applied much the same thinking to show how tightly knit communities can insulate themselves from outside pressure and sow the seeds of their own demise.[8] Or as, Portes and Landout put it: "The same strong ties that help members of a group often enable it to exclude outsiders."

Places with dense ties and high levels of traditional social capital provide advantages to insiders and thus promote stability, while places with looser networks and weaker ties are more open to newcomers, and thus promote novel combinations of resources and ideas.

Human Capital and Urban-Regional Growth

Over the past decade or so, a potentially more powerful theory for city and regional growth has emerged. This theory postulates that people are the motor force behind regional growth. Its proponents thus refer to it as the *human capital* theory of regional development.

Economists and geographers have always accepted that economic growth is regional—that it is driven by, and spreads from, specific regions, cities, or even neighborhoods. The traditional view, however, is that places grow either because they are located on transportation routes or because they have endowments of natural resources that encourage firms to locate there. According to this conventional view, the economic importance of a place is tied to the efficiency with which one can make things and do business. Governments employ this theory when they use tax breaks and highway construction to attract business. But these cost-related factors are no longer crucial to success.

The proponents of the human capital theory argue that the key to regional growth lies not in reducing the costs of doing business, but in endowments of highly educated and productive people. The human capital theory—like many theories of cities and urban areas—owes a debt to Jane Jacobs' decades-old insight that cities are uniquely positioned to attract creative people, who in turn help spur economic growth.[9] The Nobel-prize winning economist Robert Lucas sees the productivity effects that come from the clustering of human capital as the critical factor in regional economic growth, referring to this as a *Jane Jacobs externality*. Building on Jacobs' seminal insight, Lucas contends that cities would be economically unfeasible if not for the productivity effects associated with endowments of human capital. He writes:

> If we postulate only the usual list of economic forces, cities should fly apart. The theory of production contains nothing to hold a city together. A city is simply a collection of factors of production—capital, people, and land—and land is always far cheaper outside cities than inside . . . It seems to me that the *force* we need to postulate to account for the central role of cities in economic life is of exactly the same character as the *external human capital* . . . What can people be paying Manhattan or downtown Chicago rents for, if not for being near other people?[10]

Studies of national growth find a clear connection between the economic success of nations and their human capital, as measured by the level of education. This connection has also been found in regional studies of the United States. In a series of studies, Harvard University economist Edward Glaeser and his collaborators have found considerable empirical evidence that human capital is the central factor in regional growth.[11] According to Glaeser, such clustering of human capital is the ultimate source of regional agglomerations of firms: Firms concentrate to reap the advantages that stem from common labor pools—not to tap the advantages from linked networks of customers and suppliers (as is more typically argued). Research by one of Glaeser's graduate students, Spencer Glendon, shows that a good deal of city growth over the twentieth century can be traced to those cities' levels of human capital at the beginning of the century.[12] Places with greater numbers of talented people grew faster and were better able to attract more talent.

The Creative Capital Perspective

The human capital theory establishes that creative people are the driving force in regional economic growth. From that perspective, economic growth will occur in places that have highly educated people. This theory begs the question: Why do creative people cluster in certain places? In a world where people are highly mobile, why do they choose some cities over others and for what reasons?

While economists and social scientists have paid a lot of attention to how companies decide where to locate, they have virtually ignored how people do so. This is the fundamental question I sought to answer. In my interviews and focus groups, the same response kept coming back: People said that economic and lifestyle considerations *both* matter, and so does the mix of these two factors. In reality, people were not making the career decisions or geographic moves that the standard theories said they should: They were not slavishly following jobs to places. Instead, it appeared that highly educated individuals were drawn to places that were inclusive and diverse. Not only did my qualitative research indicate this trend, but the statistical analysis proved the same.

Gradually, I came to see my perspective, the Creative Capital theory, as distinct from the human capital theory. From my perspective, creative people power regional economic growth, and these people prefer places that are innovative, diverse, and tolerant. It thus differs from the human capital theory in two respects: (1) it identifies a type of human capital, creative people, as being key to economic growth; and (2) it identifies the underlying factors that shape the location decisions of these people, instead of merely saying that regions are blessed with certain endowments of them.

To begin with, Creative Capital begins most fundamentally with people: those I call the Creative Class. The distinguishing characteristic of the Creative Class is that its members engage in work whose function is to *create meaningful new forms.* The super-creative core of this new class includes scientists and engineers, university professors, poets and novelists, artists, entertainers, actors, designers, and architects, as well as the thought leadership of modern society: nonfiction writers, editors, cultural figures, think-tank researchers, analysts, and other opinion-makers. Members of this super-creative core produce new forms or designs that are readily transferable and broadly useful—such as designing a product that can be widely made, sold, and used, coming up with a theorem or strategy that can be applied in many cases, or composing music that can be performed again and again.

Beyond this core group, the Creative Class also includes creative professionals who work in a wide range of knowledge-intensive industries such as high-tech sectors, financial services, the legal and health-care professions, and business management. These people engage in creative problem-solving, drawing on complex bodies of knowledge in seeking innovative solutions. Doing so typically requires a high degree of formal education, and thus a high level of human capital. People who do this kind of work may sometimes come up with methods or products that turn out to be widely useful, but it's not part of their basic job descriptions. What they are required to do regularly is think on their own. They apply or combine standard approaches in unique ways to fit the situation, exercise a great deal of judgment, and at times must independently try new ideas and innovations on their own.

According to my estimates, the Creative Class now includes some 38.3 million Americans, roughly 30 percent of the entire U.S. work-force—up from just 10 percent at the turn of the twentieth century, and less than 20 percent as recently as 1980. It is important to point out, however, that my theory recognizes creativity as a fundamental and in-trinsic human characteristic. In a real sense, all human beings are cre-ative and all are potentially members of the Creative Class. It is just that 38 million people—roughly 30 percent of the workforce—are for-tunate enough to be paid to use their creativity regularly in their work.

In my research, I have discovered a number of trends that are in-dicative of the new geography of creativity. These are some of the key ones:

- The Creative Class is moving away from traditional corporate communities, working-class centers, and even many Sunbelt re-gions to a set of places I call *Creative Centers.*
- The Creative Centers tend to be the economic winners of our age. Not only do they have high concentrations of Creative Class peo-ple, but they boast high concentrations of creative economic out-comes, in the form of innovations and high-tech industry growth. They also show strong signs of overall regional vitality, such as in-creases in regional employment and population.
- The Creative Centers are not thriving for such traditional eco-nomic reasons as access to natural resources or transportation routes. Nor are they thriving because their local governments have gone bankrupt giving tax breaks and other incentives to lure busi-ness. They are succeeding largely because creative people want to live there. The companies follow the people—or, in many cases, are started by them. Creative Centers provide the integrated eco-system or habitat where all forms of creativity—artistic and cul-tural, technological and economic—can take root and flourish.
- Creative people are not moving to these places for traditional rea-sons. The physical attractions that most cities focus on building —sports stadiums, freeways, urban malls, and tourism-and-entertainment districts that resemble theme parks—are irrelevant,

insufficient, or actually unattractive to many Creative Class people. What they look for in communities are abundant high-quality experiences, an openness to diversity of all kinds, and above all else the opportunity to validate their identities as creative people.

The New Geography of Creativity

These shifts are giving rise to powerful migratory trends and an emerging new economic geography. In the leading Creative Centers, regions such as greater Washington, D.C., Boston, the Raleigh-Durham area, and Austin, the Creative Class makes up more than 35 percent of the workforce. But despite their considerable advantages, large regions have not cornered the market as Creative Class locations. In fact, a number of smaller regions have some of the highest creative-class concentrations in the nation—notably college towns like East Lansing, Michigan, and Madison, Wisconsin.

At the other end of the spectrum are regions that are being bypassed by the Creative Class. Among large regions, Las Vegas, Grand Rapids, and Memphis harbor the smallest concentrations of the Creative Class. Members of the Creative Class have nearly abandoned a wide range of smaller regions in the outskirts of the South and Midwest. In small metropolitan areas like Victoria, Texas, and Jackson, Tennessee, the Creative Class comprises less than 15 percent of the workforce. The leading centers for the working class among large regions are Greensboro, North Carolina, and Memphis, Tennessee, where the working-class makes up more than 30 percent of the workforce. Several smaller regions in the South and Midwest are veritable working-class enclaves with 40 to 50 percent or more of their workforce in the traditional industrial occupations.

These places have some of the most minuscule concentrations of the Creative Class in the nation. They are indicative of a general lack of overlap between the major Creative-Class centers and those of the working class. Of the 26 large cities where the working class comprises more than one-quarter of the population, only one, Houston, ranks among the top 10 destinations for the Creative Class.

Las Vegas has the highest concentration of the service class among large cities, 58 percent, while West Palm Beach, Orlando, and Miami also have around half. These regions rank near the bottom of the list for the Creative Class. The service class makes up more than half the workforce in nearly 50 small and medium-sized regions across the country. Few of them boast any significant concentrations of the Creative Class, save vacationers, and offer little prospect for upward mobility. They include resort towns like Honolulu and Cape Cod. But they also include places like Shreveport, Louisiana, and Pittsfield, Massachusetts. For these places that are not tourist destinations, the economic and social future is troubling.

Places that are home to large concentrations of the Creative Class tend to rank highly as centers of innovation and high-tech industry. Three of the top five large Creative Class regions are among the top five high-tech regions. Three of the top five large Creative Class regions are also among the top five most innovative regions (measured as patents granted per capita). And the same five large regions top the list on the Talent Index (measures as the percentage of people with a bachelor's degree or above) and Creative Class concentration: Washington, D.C., Boston, Austin, the Research Triangle, and San Francisco. My statistical correlations comparing Creative Class locations to rates of patenting and high-tech industry are uniformly positive and statistically significant.[13]

The 3 T's of Economic Growth

The key to understanding the new geography of creativity and its effects on economic outcomes lies in what I call the *3 T's* of economic development: *Technology, Talent,* and *Tolerance.* Creativity and the members of the Creative Class take root in places that possess all three of these critical factors. Each is a necessary, but by itself insufficient, condition. To attract creative people, generate innovation, and stimulate economic development, a place must have all three. I define tolerance as openness, inclusiveness, and diversity to all ethnicities, races, and walks of life. Talent is defined as those with a bachelor's degree and above. And technology is a function of both innovation and high technology concentrations in a region. My focus group and interview results indicate that talented individuals are drawn to places that offer tolerant work and social environments. The statistical analysis validates not only the focus group results, but also indicates strong relationships between technology, tolerance, and talent.

The 3 T's explain why cities like Baltimore, St. Louis, and Pittsburgh fail to grow despite their deep reservoirs of technology and world-class universities: they are unwilling to be sufficiently tolerant and open to attract and retain top creative talent. The interdependence of the 3 T's also explains why cities like Miami and New Orleans do not make the grade even though they are lifestyle meccas: they lack the required technology base. The most successful places—the San Francisco Bay Area, Boston, Washington, D.C., Austin, and Seattle—put all 3 T's together. They are truly creative places.

My colleagues and I have conducted a great deal of statistical research to test the Creative Capital theory, by looking at the way these 3 T's work together to power economic growth. We found that talent or Creative Capital is attracted to places that score high on our basic indicators of diversity—the Gay, Bohemian, and other indices. It is not because high-tech industries are populated by great numbers of bohemians and gay people. Rather, artists, musicians, gay people, and the members of the Creative Class in general prefer places that are open and diverse. Such low-entry barriers are especially important because today, places grow not just through higher birth rates (in fact virtually all U.S. cities are declining on this measure), but by their ability to attract people from the outside.

As we have already seen, human capital theorists have shown that economic growth is closely associated with concentrations of highly educated people. But few studies have specifically looked at the relationship between talent and technology, between clusters of educated and creative people and concentrations of innovation and high-tech industry. Using our measure of the Creative Class and the basic Talent Index, we examined these relationships for both the 49 regions with more than one million people and for all 206 regions for which data are available. As well as the obvious technology centers, smaller college and university towns—places like Santa Fe, Madison, Champaign-Urbana, State College and Bloomington, Indiana—rank highly on the Talent Index. When I looked at the sub-regional level, Ann Arbor (part of the Detroit region) and Boulder (part of the Denver region) rank first and third, respectively.

These findings show that both innovation and high-tech industry are strongly associated with locations of the Creative Class and of talent in general. Consider that 13 of the top 20 high-tech regions also rank among the top 20 Creative Class centers. Furthermore, an astounding 17 of the top 20 Talent Index regions also rank in the top 20 of the Creative Class. The statistical correlations between Talent Index and the Creative Class centers are understandably among the strongest of any variables in my analysis because Creative Class people tend to have high levels of education. But the correlations between Talent and Working Class regions are just the opposite—negative and highly significant—suggesting that Working Class regions possess among the lowest levels of human capital.[14]

Thus, the Creative Capital theory says that regional growth comes from the 3 T's of economic development, and to spur innovation and economic growth a region must emphasize all three.

The Role of Diversity

Economists have long argued that diversity is important to economic performance, but they have usually meant the diversity of firms or industries. The economist John Quigley, for instance, argues that regional economies benefit from the location of a diverse set of firms and industries.[15] Jacobs long ago highlighted the role of diversity of both firms and people in powering innovation and city growth. As she saw it, great cities are places where people from virtually any background are welcome to turn their energy and ideas into innovations and wealth.[16]

This raises an interesting question. Does living in an open and diverse environment help to make talented and creative people even more productive; or do its members simply cluster around one another and thus drive up these places' creativity only as a by-product? I believe both are going on, but the former is more important. Places that are open and possess *low barriers to entry* for people gain creativity advantage from their ability to attract people from a wide range of backgrounds. All else being equal, more open and diverse places are likely to attract greater numbers of talented and creative people—the sort of people who power innovation and growth.

Low Barriers to Entry

A large number of studies point to the role of immigrants in economic development. In *The Global Me,* Pascal Zachary argues that openness to immigration is the cornerstone of innovation and economic growth. He contends that America's successful economic performance is directly linked to its openness to innovative and energetic people from around the world, and attributes the decline of once prospering countries, such as Japan and Germany, to the homogeneity of their populations.[17]

My team and I examined the relationships between immigration or percent foreign-born and high-tech industry. Inspired by a Milken Institute study that measures regional concentrations of high technology industry—the Tech-Pole index—we dubbed this the Melting Pot Index. The effect of openness to immigration on regions is mixed. Four out of the top 10 regions on the Melting Pot Index are also among the nation's top 10 high-technology areas; seven of the top 10 are in the top 25 high-tech regions. The Melting Pot Index is positively associated with the Tech-Pole Index statistically. Clearly, as UC-Berkeley professor Annalee Saxenian argues, immigration is associated with high-tech industry. But immigration is not strongly associated with innovation. The Melting Pot Index is not statistically correlated with the Innovation Index, measured as rates of patenting. Although it is positively associated with population growth, it is not correlated with job growth.[18] Furthermore, places that are open to immigration do not necessarily number among the leading Creative Class Centers. While 12 of the top 20 Melting Pot regions number in the top 20 centers for the Creative Class, no significant statistical relationship exists between the Melting Pot Index and the Creative Class.[19]

The Gay Index

While immigrants may be important to regional growth, other types of diversity exist that statistically prove even more important. In the late 1990s, the Urban Institute's Gary Gates used information from the U.S. Census of Population to figure out where gay couples located. He discovered that particular cities were favorites among the gay population.

The results of our statistical analysis on the gay population are squarely in line with the Creative Capital theory. The Gay Index is strongly associated with a region's high-tech industry concentration. Six of the top 10 1990 and five of top 10 2000 Gay Index regions also rank among the nations top 10 high-tech regions. In virtually all of our statistical analysis, the Gay Index did better than any other individual measure of diversity as a predictor of high-tech industry.[20] Gays not only predict the concentration of high-tech industry, they also predict its growth. Four of the regions that rank in the top 10 for high-technology growth from 1990 to 1998 also rank in the top ten on the Gay Index in both 1990 and 2000.[21] In addition, the correlation between the Gay Index (measured in 1990) and the Tech-Pole Index, calculated for 1990 to 2000, increases over time. This suggests that the benefits of diversity may actually compound.

Several reasons exist why the Gay Index is a good measure for diversity. As a group, gays have been subject to a particularly high level of discrimination. Attempts by gays to integrate into the mainstream of society have met substantial opposition. To some extent, homosexuality represents the last frontier of diversity in our society, and thus a place that welcomes the gay community welcomes all kinds of people.[22]

The Bohemian Index

As early as the 1920 studies by Robert Park, sociologists have observed the link between successful cities and the prevalence of bohemian culture. Working with my Carnegie Mellon team, I developed a new measure, called the *Bohemian Index*, that uses census occupation data to measure the number of writers, designers, musicians, actors, directors, painters, sculptors, photographers, and dancers in a region. The Bohemian Index is an improvement over traditional measures of amenities because it directly counts the producers of the amenities using reliable census data. In addition to large regions such as San Francisco, Boston, Seattle, and Los Angeles, smaller communities like Boulder and Fort Collins, Colorado; Sarasota, Florida; Santa Barbara, California; and Madison, Wisconsin rank rather highly when all regions are taken into account.

The Bohemian Index turns out to be an amazingly strong predictor of everything from a region's high-technology base to its overall population and employment growth.[23] Five of the top 10 and 12 of the top

20 Bohemian Index regions number among the nation's top 20 high-technology regions. Eleven of the top 20 Bohemian Index regions number among the top 20 most innovative regions.[24] The Bohemian Index is also a strong predictor of both regional employment and population growth. A region's Bohemian presence in 1990 predicts both its high-tech industry concentration and its employment and population growth between 1990 and 2000.

Testing the Theories

Robert Cushing, the University of Texas statistician, has systematically tested the three major theories of regional growth: social capital, human capital, and creative capital. In a nutshell, Cushing finds that social capital theory provide little explanation for regional growth. Both the human capital and creative capital theories are much better at accounting for such growth. Furthermore, he finds that creative communities and social capital communities are moving in opposite directions. Creative communities are centers of diversity, innovation, and economic growth; social capital communities are not.

Cushing went to great pains to replicate Putnam's data sources. He looked at the surveys conducted by a team that, under Putnam's direction, did extensive telephone interviewing in 40 cities to gauge the depth and breadth of social capital. Based on the data, Putnam measured 13 different kinds of social capital and gave each region a score for attributes like *political involvement, civic leadership, faith-based institutions, protest politics,* and *giving and volunteering.* Using Putnam's own data, Cushing found little evidence of a decline in volunteering. Rather, he found that volunteering was up in recent years. People were more likely to engage in volunteer activity in the late 1990s than they were in the 1970s. Volunteering by men was 5.8 percent higher in the 5-year period 1993 to 1998 than it had been in the period 1975 to 1980. Volunteering by women was up by 7.6 percent. A variety of statistical tests confirmed these results, but Cushing did not stop there. He then combined this information on social capital trends with independent data on high-tech industry, innovation, human capital, and diversity. He added the Milken Institute's Tech-Pole Index, the Innovation Index, and measures of talent, diversity, and creativity (the Talent Index, the Gay Index, and the Bohemian Index.) He grouped the regions according to the Tech-Pole Index and the Innovation Index (their ability to produce patents).

Cushing found that regions ranked high on the Milken Tech-Pole Index and Innovation Index ranked low on 11 of Putnam's 13 measures of social capital. High-tech regions scored below average on almost every measure of social capital. High-tech regions had less trust, less reliance on faith-based institutions, fewer clubs, less volunteering, less interest in traditional politics, and less civic leadership. The two measures of social capital where these regions excelled were *protest politics* and *diversity of friendships.* Regions low on the Tech-Pole Index and the Innovation Index were exactly the opposite. They scored high on 11 of the 13 Putnam measures but below average on *protest politics* and *diversity.* Cushing then threw into the mix individual wages, income distribution, population growth, numbers of college-educated residents, and scientists and engineers. He found that the high-tech regions had higher incomes, more growth, more income inequality, and more scientists, engineers, and professions than their low-tech, but higher social capital counterparts. When Cushing compared the Gay and Bohemian indices to Putnam's measures of social capital in the 40 regions surveyed in 2000, the same basic pattern emerged: Regions high on these two diversity indices were low on 11 of 13 of Putnam's categories of social capital. In Cushing's words, "conventional political involvement and social capital seem to relate negatively to technological development and higher economic growth." Based on this analysis, Cushing identified four distinct types of communities. While the analysis is Cushing's, the labels are my own.

Classic Social Capital Communities: These are the places that best fit the Putnam theory—places like Bismarck, North Dakota; rural South Dakota; Baton Rouge, Louisiana; Birmingham, Alabama; and Greensboro, Charlotte, and Winston-Salem, North Carolina. They score high on social capital and political involvement but low on diversity, innovation, and high-tech industry.

Organizational Age Communities: These are older, corporate-dominated communities like Cleveland, Detroit, Grand Rapids, and Kalamazoo. They have average social capital, higher-than-average political involvement, low levels of diversity, and low levels of innovation and high-tech industry. They score high on my Working Class Index. In my view, they represent the classic corporate centers of the organizational age.

Nerdistans: Fast-growing regions like Silicon Valley, San Diego, Phoenix, Atlanta, Los Angeles, and Houston—lauded by some as models of rapid economic growth but seen by others as plagued with sprawl, pollution, and congestion. These regions have lots of high-tech industry, above average diversity, low social capital, and low political involvement.

Creative Centers: These large urban centers, such as San Francisco, Seattle, Boston, Chicago, Minneapolis, Denver, and Boulder, have high levels of innovation and high-tech industry and high levels of diversity but lower than average levels of social capital and moderate levels of political involvement. These cities score highly on my Creativity Index and are repeatedly identified in my focus groups and interviews as desirable places to live and work. That's why I see them as representing the new creative mainstream.

In winter 2001, Cushing extended his analysis to include more than three decades of data for one hundred regions. Again, he based his analysis on Putnam's own data sources: the 30-year time series collected by DDB Worldwide, the advertising firm, on activities such as church going, participation in clubs and committees, volunteer activity, and entertaining people at home. He used these data to group the regions into high and low social capital communities, and found that social capital had little to do with regional economic growth. The high social capital communities showed a strong preference for *social isolation* and *security and stability* and grew the least—their defining attribute being a *close the gates* mentality. The low social capital communities had the highest rates of diversity and population growth.

Finally, Cushing undertook an objective and systematic comparison of the effect of the three theories—social capital, human capital, and creative capital—on economic growth. He built statistical models to determine the effect of these factors on population growth (a well-accepted measure of regional growth) between 1990 and 2000. To do so, he included separate measures of education and human capital, occupation, wages and hours worked, poverty and income inequality, innovation and high-tech industry, and creativity and diversity for the period 1970 to 1990.

Again his results were striking. He found no evidence that social capital leads to regional economic growth; in fact, the effects were negative. Both the human capital and creative capital models performed much better, according to his analysis. Turning first to the human capital approach, he found that, while it did a good job of accounting for regional growth, "the interpretation is not as straightforward as the human capital approach might presume." Using creative occupations, bohemians, the Tech-Pole Index, and innovations as indicators of creative capital, he found the creative capital theory produced formidable results, with the predictive power of the Bohemian and Innovation Indices being particularly high, concluding that the "creative capital model generates equally impressive results as the human capital model, and perhaps better."[25]

In the chapters that follow, we will explore in greater depth what it takes for cities to succeed. Alongside this, we will tease out the particular components responsible for the success—or lack thereof—of cities in today's creative economy. There exist many factors, and some of these factors cut against the grain of traditional ideas about urban innovation. But detailed analyses of the engines that are drawing talent to particular places make the process quite clear: talent migrates to regions possessing high degrees of social openness, diversity, and creativity. Regional economic dynamism results.

PART I
TALENT

3

COMPETING IN THE AGE OF TALENT

The creative economy is reshaping nearly every aspect of economic development as we know it. Knowledge and creativity have replaced natural resources and the efficiency of physical labor as the sources of wealth creation and economic growth. In this new era, human capital, or talent, has become the key factor of production.[1]

The rise of this creative economy radically alters the ways that cities and regions establish and maintain competitive advantage.[2] The key to success in the industrial age was simple—the overall costs of doing business. In the mass production era, regions established competitive advantage via natural advantages in resource endowments, transportation access, the cost and productivity of physical labor, and by reducing overall cost. Driven to reduce, firms selected locations that provided low cost land, cheap or highly productive physical labor, and a cost-conscious business climate. Regional development strategies typically emphasized the use of so-called business incentives designed to win over businesses by pushing their costs even lower. The environment and natural amenities were seen merely as sources of raw materials or as places to dispose wastes.

In the creative economy, regional advantage comes to places that can quickly mobilize the talent, resources, and capabilities required to turn innovations into new business ideas and commercial products. Leading regions establish competitive advantage through their capabilities. They are vehicles for mobilization that can almost instantaneously bring together the resources required to launch new businesses and turn innovations into successful products. For these reasons, the nexus of competitive advantage shifts to those regions that can generate, retain, and attract the best talent. This is particularly true because creative workers are extremely mobile and the distribution of talent is highly skewed.

Today, it is the ability to attract human capital or talent that creates regional advantage: Those that have the talent win, those that do not lose. In this regard, the *quality* of place, a city or region, has replaced access as the pivot point of competitive advantage. Quality-of-place features attractive to talented workers of a region have thus become central to regional strategies for developing high-tech industries.

For regional development strategy, this means a shift from low cost to high quality—from merely attracting firms to forming the coalitions that are required to generate, retain, and attract talent. For instance, the rise of the creative economy dramatically transforms the role of the environment and natural amenities—from a source of raw materials and a sink for waste disposal to a critical component of the total package required to attract talent. In doing so, it generates economic growth.

The location decisions of creative people—that is, how new people in technology-based and professional occupations choose places to live and work—tell us a great deal about how regions attract talent in the creative economy. As it turns out, amenities and the environment have proven to be powerful attractors of creative workers. In turn, they have aided the development of high-technology industries and regions.

Understanding the connections between talent, place, and creative economy success, though, requires answering an ensemble of questions. What are the primary factors that shape the location decisions of creative workers or talent? Traditionally, market factors such as the availability of jobs or careers have been thought to dominate these decisions. They obviously remain important, but what role do place-based factors such as lifestyle, environmental quality, and amenities now play in these choices? And how does this affect the process of economic development more generally?

High-Technology Regions

Before answering these questions about the role of place in the creative economy, however, it is useful to identify the leading regions of the creative economy.

Numerous ways exist to define high-technology regions, and such definitional issues have been the subject of considerable debate among academics and professional analysts. A 1999 report by the Milken Institute provides a careful and comprehensive rating of 350 U.S. regions across several dimensions of high technology, making it the best available summary ranking of high-technology regions.[3] Table 3.1 provides overall Milken *tech-pole* scores and ranks for 35 benchmark regions. This tech-pole score is a composite of several measures of high-technology concentration and growth. Not surprisingly, the most highly ranked region was San Jose—California's Silicon Valley—followed by Dallas, Texas; Boston, Massachusetts; Seattle, Washington; and Washington, D.C.

It is also useful to compare the Milken rankings to other rankings of high-technology regions. Table 3.2 provides a listing of *Forbes* leading technology regions and Table 3.3 lists the most wired cities. While the specific regional rankings vary, there is considerable overlap between these lists. Seattle, Washington; Austin, Texas; Dallas, Texas; Ventura, California; and Oakland, California top the list of Forbes' best cities for technology business,[4] while San Francisco, Atlanta, Washington, D.C., Austin, Seattle, Minneapolis, and Boston top the list of *wired* cities.[5]

In addition to knowing which regions are leading centers of high technology industry, it is also important to know which regions are able to attract talent. Table 3.4 provides several measures of talent for the benchmark regions. This analysis uses workers in the software industry as a proxy for talent.[6] To control for the different sizes of various regions, Table 3.4 ranks regions by the number of software workers per million population. It also presents the total number of software workers, the change in software workers between 1991 and 1996, the overall rate of change or growth rate, and the average annual rate of change over this period.

Table 3.1 High Technology Rankings for Benchmark Regions

RANK AMONG BENCHMARK REGIONS	CITY	SCORE	OVERALL RANK
1	San Jose	23.686	1
2	Dallas–Fort Worth	7.063	2
3	Boston	6.308	4
4	Seattle	5.191	5
5	Washington	5.078	6
6	Albuquerque	4.978	7
7	Atlanta	3.462	10
8	Phoenix–Mesa	2.604	12
9	Oakland	2.213	14
10	Philadelphia	2.192	15
11	Rochester	1.953	16
12	San Diego	1.932	17
13	Raleigh–Durham	1.892	18
14	Denver	1.812	19
15	Austin–San Marcos	1.775	21
16	San Francisco	1.623	22
17	Houston	1.621	23
18	Boise City	1.427	24
19	New Haven	1.333	25
20	Portland–Salem–Vancouver	1.333	26
21	Boulder	1.123	27
22	Kalamazoo	1.093	28
23	Indianapolis	1.070	29
24	Kansas City	1.034	31
25	Minneapolis–St. Paul	0.981	32
26	Lubbock	0.967	33
27	St. Louis	0.927	34
28	Cedar Rapids	0.916	35
29	Orlando	0.822	36
30	Detroit	0.790	38
31	Pittsburgh	0.482	47
32	Tampa–St. Petersburg	0.420	51
33	Baltimore	0.357	68
34	Cleveland–Akron	0.225	69
35	Miami–Ft. Lauderdale	0.240	70.5

Source: Ross C. DeVol, *America's High Technology Economy,* 1999

Leading high-tech regions—San Jose, Washington, D.C., San Francisco, and Boston—top the list in terms of software workers per million people, followed by Atlanta, Dallas, and Denver. Kansas City,

Table 3.2 Forbes Best Places Top 15

RANK	CITY	RANK	CITY
1	Seattle, WA	9	Houston, TX
2	Austin, TX	10	Atlanta, GA
3	Dallas, TX	11	Orange County, CA
4	Ventura, CA	12	San Diego, CA
5	Oakland, CA	13	Omaha, NE
6	Somerset, NJ	14	Santa Rosa, CA
7	Denver, CO	15	Tampa, FL
8	San Jose, CA		

Source: *Forbes* magazine, 1999

Table 3.3 America's Most Wired Cities

RANK	CITY
1	San Francisco
2	Atlanta
3	Washington
4	Austin
5	Seattle
6	Minneapolis–St. Paul
7	Boston
8	New York
9	Chicago
10	Miami
11	Denver
12	San Diego
13	Dallas
14	Pittsburgh
15	St. Louis

Source: *Yahoo! Internet Life* magazine, http://www.zdnet.com/yil/content/mag/9803/

Austin, Denver, and Oakland had average annual growth rates of software workers in excess of 20 percent. Atlanta, Seattle, Tampa, Orlando, Phoenix, San Francisco, and Boston had average annual creative worker growth rates of roughly 15 percent or more.

Figure 3.1 compares regions by their ability to generate and attract software workers and concentrations of high-technology industry. Regions that place in the far upper right-hand quadrant of these charts are in a win-win position, scoring well in both the growth of creative workers and in the concentration of high-technology industries.

Table 3.4 Software Workers in Benchmark Regions

REGION	PER MILLION	NUMBER	CHANGE (91–96)	RATE OF CHANGE (91–96)	ANNUAL RATE
San Jose, CA	24348.74	38818	14039	56.66%	11.33%
Washington, DC	22561.95	102652	33249	47.91%	9.58%
San Francisco, CA	17632.61	29147	12930	79.73%	15.95%
Boston, MA	16871.44	54959	23346	73.85%	14.77%
Atlanta, GA	11633.74	41098	19849	93.41%	18.68%
Dallas–Fort Worth, TX	11345.50	51692	18268	54.66%	10.93%
Denver, CO	11258.22	20964	11337	117.76%	23.55%
Oakland, CA	9700.85	21703	11058	103.88%	20.78%
Minneapolis–St. Paul, MN	9407.78	25976	10702	70.07%	14.01%
Raleigh–Durham, NC	9308.79	9512	2526	36.16%	7.23%
Austin–San Marcos, TX	9156.99	9511	5159	118.54%	23.71%
Seattle–Bellevue–Everett, WA	8365.94	18663	8912	91.40%	18.28%
Detroit, MI	7337.06	32717	12786	64.15%	12.83%
Tampa–St. Petersburg, FL	6872.22	15086	6858	83.35%	16.67%
Orlando, FL	5986.83	8509	3754	78.95%	15.79%
San Diego, CA	5953.73	15918	5349	50.61%	10.12%
St. Louis, MO	5632.89	14363	4050	39.27%	7.85%
Philadelphia, PA	5552.37	27475	5824	26.90%	5.38%
Houston, TX	5171.45	19497	4395	29.10%	5.82%
Portland, OR	5160.55	9053	1568	20.95%	4.19%
Indianapolis, IN	4703.72	7005	2000	39.96%	7.99%
Pittsburgh, PA	4272.07	10143	3950	63.78%	12.76%
Baltimore, MD	4224.04	10429	2554	32.43%	6.49%
Kansas City, MO	4069.50	6897	3983	136.68%	27.34%
Phoenix–Mesa, AZ	3927.91	10815	5394	99.50%	19.90%
Cleveland–Akron, OH	3740.38	10906	3380	44.91%	8.98%
Miami–Ft. Lauderdale, FL	3207.01	11372	4143	57.31%	11.46%

Source: County Business Patterns, various years

Regions in the lower left-hand quadrant are laggards on both dimensions.

Leading high-technology centers such as San Jose, Boston, and Washington, D.C., top the list in terms of this joint measure, placing in the far upper right-hand quadrant of this graph. Dallas, Atlanta, Seattle, Oakland, Denver, San Francisco, Raleigh-Durham, and Austin also score relatively highly on this measure. Regions such as Cleveland, Baltimore, St. Louis, Pittsburgh, and Miami occupy the lower left-hand quadrant of the chart. These regions are stragglers in both arenas.

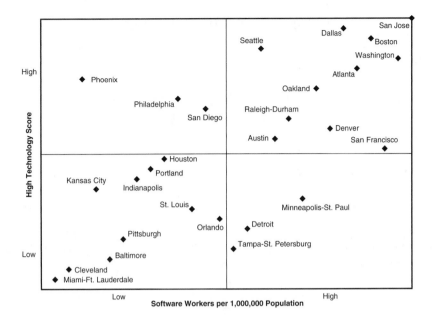

Figure 3.1 High technology and software workers

Entrepreneurship—along with high-technology industry and the ability to attract creative talent—is an essential element of regional economic growth. Table 3.5 presents the rankings of the benchmark regions in terms of entrepreneurial hot spots using the rating system developed by *Cognetics*.[7] Figure 3.2 compares high technology and entrepreneurship, and Figure 3.3 compares entrepreneurship and the growth rate for software workers for the benchmark regions. The key findings here are as follows.

- Phoenix tops the list of entrepreneurial hotspots among large regions, followed by Raleigh-Durham and Atlanta of the benchmark regions. Austin tops the list of entrepreneurial hot spots among smaller regions.
- Atlanta, Phoenix, Raleigh, Austin, Dallas, and Washington, D.C., rank highly as centers for high technology and entrepreneurship.

Table 3.5 Entrepreneurial Rankings for Benchmark Regions

LARGE REGIONS	RANK
Phoenix–Mesa	1
Raleigh–Durham	3
Atlanta	4
Indianapolis	5
Orlando	6
Dallas–Fort Worth	8
Washington	10
Denver–Boulder	11
Minneapolis–St. Paul	12
Kansas City	13
Portland–Salem–Vancouver	19
San Diego	22
St. Louis	23
Miami–Ft. Lauderdale	25
Tampa–St. Petersburg	26
Houston	27
San Francisco–Oakland–San Jose	29
Cleveland–Akron	34
Boston	36
Baltimore	37
Detroit	38
Seattle	39
Philadelphia	44
Pittsburgh	46
SMALLER REGIONS	**RANK**
Austin–San Marcos	3
Boise City	7
Cedar Rapids	29
Albuquerque	47

Source: David Birch, Anne Haggerty, and William Parsons, "Entrepreneurial Hot Spots," *Cognetics,* 1999: pp. 24, 26.

- Atlanta, Austin, Raleigh-Durham, Dallas, Washington, D.C., Denver, and Minneapolis rank highly in terms of entrepreneurship and software workers, occupying the upper right-hand quadrant of Figure 3.3.

Talent and the Environment

In the industrial economy, economic growth and the environment were typically seen to be at odds. Economic growth came at the expense of

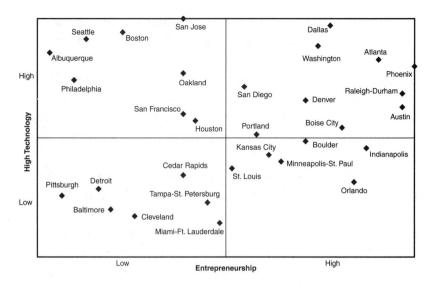

Source: www.milken-inst.org and David Birch et al, "Entrepreneurial Hot Spots," *Cognetics*

Figure 3.2 Entrepreneurship and high technology

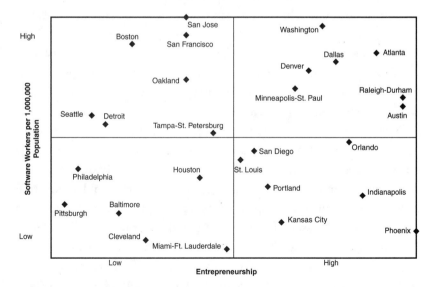

Source: County Business Patterns and David Birch et al, "Entrepreneurial Hot Spots," *Cognetics*

Figure 3.3 Entrepreneurship and software workers

environmental quality. Indeed, the environment was viewed as a source of raw material to be exploited as input for production, as a vehicle for transporting raw materials or finished goods, and as a dumping ground for waste and emissions. Industrial cities and regions suffered levels of air pollution so thick that managers would have to change their shirts at noon, and on some days the streetlights would be turned on at midday. Rivers were walled off from the population, and in some cities might even catch fire.

In the creative economy, the situation has reversed itself. Environmental quality has become important not simply as an end in itself, but as a prerequisite for attracting talent. Leading corporations have established a new relationship between the environment and economic competitiveness. These companies have pioneered new industrial systems which eliminate the century-old tradeoff between the environment and productivity, striving to achieve *three zero* production—zero defects (quality,) zero inventory (just-in-time delivery), and zero waste and emissions.[8] These companies have also improved the design and environmental quality of their facilities to attract and motivate employees. Furthermore, leading high-technology firms, such as AOL, have played and continue to play a leading role in *smart growth* movements to reduce congestion and limit urban sprawl in areas like Washington, D.C., Boston, the San Francisco Bay Area, and Seattle. These efforts have been motivated not only by altruistic concerns, but also by the bottom-line drive to increase profits, productivity, and performance by reducing waste and emissions and creating a cleaner, greener environment.

Now, forward-looking *regions* also see the environment as a source of economic competitiveness, quality-of-life, and talent attraction. They have undertaken efforts to reduce sprawl and move to smart growth, promote environmental sustainability, clean up and reuse older industrial sites, encourage firms to adopt environmental management systems, and preserve natural assets for recreation and improved quality-of-life. Chattanooga, Tennessee, for instance, has led the way in showing how regions can use environmental restoration, riverfront redevelopment, improved quality of life, and natural resources for recreation cornerstones of their economic development strategy.

Environmental Renewal as Economic Development: Chattanooga, Tennessee[9]

Chattanooga, Tennessee, has made environmental quality and sustainable development the centerpiece of its regional economic strategy. Instead of following the traditional development model of low-cost business attraction, the city has crafted a sustainable plan for development based on environmental technology research and business creation, environmental quality, preservation of natural amenities, and encouragement of smart growth. In doing so, it has become a model for sustainable economic development based on the full use of all of its resources.

Chattanooga was once known as the *Pittsburgh of the South* because of its heavy reliance on high-polluting industries for economic survival. Iron foundries, textile mills, and chemical plants formed the backbone of the city's economy. As these industries began to decline and factories closed down, the city slid into a deep recession. Today, the city has committed itself to becoming a laboratory for sustainable development programs and is often called *The Sustainable City*. Chattanooga has been recognized for its sustainable vision by being named the 10th most enlightened city in the country by *Urban Quality Indicators* in 1997 and by being named one of the best places to live by *Partners for Livable Places* in 1994. The region's economic revitalization began in 1984 with a program called Vision 2000.

Vision 2000 involved 1,700 citizens in 20 weeks of meetings to develop ideas for improving the city. The program produced 34 overall goals and 223 projects. By 1992, over 85 percent of the goals had been met, leading to a 1993 program called *ReVision 2000*, which laid out 27 more goals. These achieved goals included a revitalization of downtown with historic theaters, inns, and a waterfront park called *Riverwalk* (see following). In 1992, the Tennessee Aquarium opened. This $45 million facility attracted over 1.5 million visitors to the downtown area in its first year alone. Current plans call for a *zero-emissions industrial zone*, which would create a mixed residential-commercial district on what is now a blighted industrial area, and reusing the *Volunteer Site*, a 7,000-acre site that was once home to the world's largest TNT plant. This site is to be transformed into an ecoindustrial park.

Chattanooga's redevelopment efforts have focused on eliminating pollution and transforming once-contaminated sites into centers of outdoor recreation and natural amenities—an inclusive public process that has involved thousands of residents and businesses. For example, the city holds regular public forums on environmental issues and uses a unique *Futurescape* process that involves citizen use of videotapes to determine public preferences on land use issues.

The city's riverfront area, once heavily polluted, is being transformed into the Riverwalk, with picnic areas and a sculpture garden extending over 22 miles of riverfront, part of a projected 75 miles of greenways throughout the city. The riverfront has also been used as a site for new housing development. Riverset Apartments, the first new downtown housing development in Chattanooga in 20 years, opened in 1993 and was completely leased within 8 months of opening. The complex was built on an attractive riverfront site that offers quick access to other riverfront amenities, such as the Riverwalk and the Tennessee Aquarium.

Public transit is encouraged, and the city uses locally produced electric buses to transport residents. These electric buses have had the dual impact of alleviating air pollution and serving as an exportable product for the local business community. They are free to the public, and are subsidized from concessions from a downtown multi-screen theater. The city has high hopes for a planned high-speed rail connection to Atlanta that will cut commuting time between the two cities to 45 minutes, establishing a *Chatlanta* corridor. Chattanooga also encourages residents to walk from place to place through its emphasis on outdoor amenities. The riverpark is one example of this, and the city has also built several walking bridges connecting parks, the aquarium, an arts district, and the University of Tennessee.

Chattanooga illustrates how a once badly polluted industrial city can be revitalized by leveraging environmental renewal and a commitment to natural assets as an integral component of its economic development strategy. Chattanooga has become a model for cities looking to achieve economic success and a higher quality of life for all residents while generating improved environmental quality.

Such cities are on the right track: Surveys and other studies of high-technology businesses have found that environmental quality and natural amenities are important factors in a firm's choice of location (see Tables 3.6 and 3.7).[10] Environmental quality was the top-rated factor for firms, ranking ahead of housing costs, cost of living, commuting patterns, school climate, government services, and public safety. It rated considerably ahead of CEO preference—frequently alluded to as a key location factor for high-technology firms. But this logic doesn't apply to all firms: Environmental quality ranked considerably higher as a location factor for high technology firms than for other types. Table 3.6 illustrates the importance of environmental quality as a location factor for high-technology firms.

Examining the relationship between environmental quality, high technology, and talent for benchmark regions allows us to get a more systematic handle on the connection between environmental quality and the creative economy. A basic measure is to compare regional performance on a series of measures of environmental quality—air quality, water quality, and urban sprawl—to regional performance in terms of high-technology and talent.[11] The bottom line is that there is a considerable relationship between environmental quality, high-technology industry concentration, and talent.

Table 3.6 Environmental Quality and High Technology Location

High Technology Firms		All Firms	
AMENITY	AVERAGE SCORE	AMENITY	AVERAGE SCORE
Environmental Quality	3.00	Good Schools	2.11
Cost of Housing	3.24	Public Safety	3.89
Cost of Living	3.38	Environmental Quality	4.22
Good Schools	3.50	Cultural Amenities	4.56
Easy Commute	3.50	Proximity of Housing	4.89
Recreational Amenities	3.63	Easy Commute	4.89
Climate	3.75	Cost of Housing	5.00
Cultural Amenities	4.13	Recreational Amenities	5.22
Government Services	4.50	Climate	5.89
CEO Preference	4.50	Government Services	6.22
Public Safety	5.25	Cost of Living	6.67
Proximity of Housing	5.25	CEO Preference	6.78

Source: Paul Gottlieb, "Amenities As an Economic Development Tool: Is There Enough Evidence?" *Economic Development Quarterly*, August 1994, p. 276

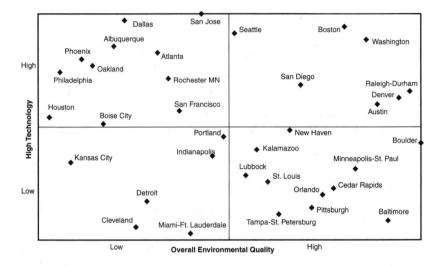

Source: www.milken-inst.org, http://www.pathfinder.com/money/bestplaces/ and www.sierraclub.org/sprawl

Figure 3.4 Environment and high technology

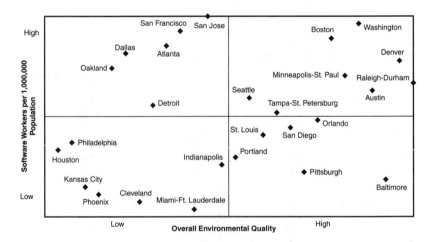

Source: County Business Patterns, www.pathfinder.com/money/bestplaces/ and www.sierraclub.org/sprawl

Figure 3.5 Environment and software workers

- Washington, D.C., Raleigh-Durham, Denver, Austin, Boston, Seattle, and San Diego rank highly in terms of both overall environmental quality and high-technology concentration, occupying the upper right-hand quadrant of Figure 3.4.
- Washington, D.C., Austin, Raleigh-Durham, Denver, Boston, Seattle, Minneapolis, and Tampa score well in terms of environmental quality and software workers, occupying the upper right-hand quadrant of Figure 3.5.
- Several high-technology regions—notably Boston, Washington, D.C., Raleigh, Denver, Austin, and Seattle—rate highly in terms of high technology and air-water quality, occupying the upper right-hand quadrant of Figure 3.6.
- The same is the case for talent, where Washington, D.C., Boston, Denver, Raleigh, Austin, Seattle, Minneapolis, and Tampa occupy the upper right-hand quadrant of Figure 3.7.

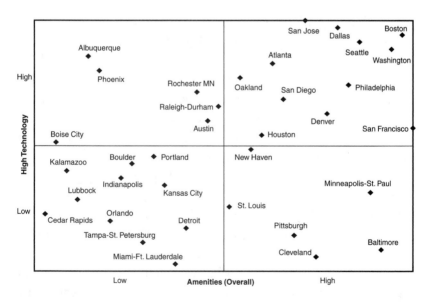

Source: www.milken-inst.org, www.pathfinder.com/money/bestplaces/, and "Boom Town USA," POV, December/January 1999, pp. 69–81

Figure 3.6 Amenities and high technology

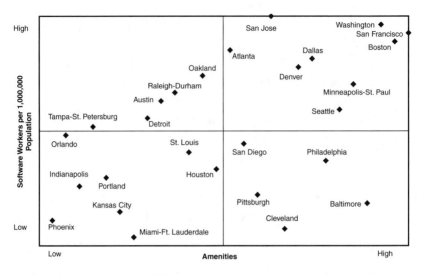

Source: County Business Patterns, www.pathfinder.com/money/bestplaces/, "Boom Town USA," *POV*, December/January 1999, pp. 69–81

Figure 3.7 Amenities and software workers

The findings with regard to sprawl, on the other hand, are mixed (see Table 3.7). A number of high technology regions have been able to develop without generating sprawl, while others are under considerable pressure to expand outward. The successful ones—notably San Jose, Boston, and San Francisco—appear to have been reasonably successful in developing a high-technology economy without putting themselves at risk for excessive urban sprawl. While traffic congestion may well be an issue in these regions, they did not make the Sierra Club's list of cities most threatened by sprawl. But several other leading high-technology regions appear to be threatened, to some degree, by such expansion. Atlanta, Seattle, Austin, Denver, Dallas, Raleigh, and Washington, D.C., all placed high on the Sierra Club's 1998 list of cities at risk for sprawl, according to the Sierra Club's ranking of *sprawl threatened* cities.

Sprawl poses a particularly vexing problem for rapidly growing high-technology regions. Part of their appeal in the first place comes from their manageable size and high quality of life. But growth generates pressures that threaten these very qualities. A rapidly growing high-technology economy brings with it social and environmental costs as a

Table 3.7 Sprawl Rankings for Benchmark Regions

REGION	Large (1 million and over) SPRAWL RISK RANK
Atlanta	1
St. Louis	2
Washington	3
Cincinnati	4
Kansas City	5
Denver	6
Seattle	7
Minneapolis–St. Paul	8
Ft. Lauderdale	9
Chicago	10
Detroit	11
Baltimore	12
Cleveland	13
Tampa	14
Dallas	15
Hampton Roads	16
Pittsburgh	17
Miami	18
San Antonio	19
Riverside/San Bernardino	20

REGION	Medium (500,000–1 million) SPRAWL RISK RANK
Orlando	1
Austin	2
Las Vegas	3
West Palm Beach	4
Akron	5

REGION	Small (200,000–500,000) SPRAWL RISK RANK
McAllen, TX	1
Raleigh, NC	2
Pensacola, FL	3
Daytona Beach, FL	4
Little Rock, AR	5

REGION	Dishonorable Mentions SPRAWL RISK RANK
Los Angeles	1
San Diego	2
Phoenix	3

Source: The Sierra Club, www.sierraclub.org/sprawl/report98/map.html

consequence of greater industrial activity and population growth. Deteriorating air quality, traffic congestion, and damage to natural amenities are some of the negative outcomes that challenge prospering high-technology regions. In extreme cases, unmanaged growth may eventually destroy the appeal of a region, create an impediment to growth, and make other regions relatively more attractive location choices.

A number of high-technology regions are, however, taking active steps to try to address the challenges created by sprawl, introducing smart-growth campaigns and sustainable development strategies. Seattle, for instance, has developed a strong sustainability agenda. Portland has implemented a smart-growth strategy and in some instances tied the expansion of high technology plants to environmental considerations. The city has also instituted a program of financial penalties designed to discourage excessive growth by one of its largest employers, Intel, Inc. Intel has said that it expects to create fewer than 1,000 manufacturing jobs over the next 15 years. If the company exceeds that target, it must pay the county a fine of $1,000 per year for each additional employee. Austin, Texas, has made smart-growth one of two pillars of its high technology economic strategy—the other being the continued development of its high technology clusters.

SMART GROWTH AND AUSTIN'S HIGH-TECHNOLOGY STRATEGY[12]

Austin, Texas, has developed a two-pronged strategy for its economic future: high technology and smart growth along with lifestyle amenities. In 1998, the Greater Austin Chamber of Commerce undertook a new regional strategy outlined in a report entitled *Next Century Economy*. This report examined where Austin had come from in its economic turn-around and where it needed to go to sustain that economic prosperity. It outlined a vision for *creating sustainable advantage*. The report identified three strategies for the city to follow in developing sustainable advantage.

The first strategy involved bolstering the region's already thriving high-technology economy by (1) improving communication between the region's economic clusters and their suppliers, (2) improving the economic foundations of existing businesses, (3) leveraging cluster-based R&D at the University of Texas, and (4) attracting firms to complement existing industries by filling supply gaps in existing clusters.

The second strategy called for the region to "ensure environmental quality and social opportunity by explicitly linking social and environmental goals to economic development goals." This strategy called for programs to protect the region's high quality of life from the pressures created by rapid economic growth. Additionally, the report called for more effective land use and transportation planning by linking planning processes to the needs of cluster industries to maximize their future growth. As the report argued, "addressing social and environmental issues [is] also increasingly key to maintaining support for future growth."

The third strategy involved developing a regional collaborative mechanism for major problem-solving, in particular for linking high-technology development to smart growth and amenities.

The report outlined the strategy as follows:

A clean and well-managed environment and an economy that provides job opportunities for all its residents, are important community objectives. But given Austin's economic direction, environmental and social issues are important for a second reason: They are also critical inputs to its long-term economic competitiveness. If Austin's robust technology-driven economy has one weakness, it is a chronic labor shortage in technical fields . . . Similarly, if Austin is to keep its skilled workforce and continue to attract people from other regions, it will have to offer more than high wages—many regions can offer high wages. The region will need to leverage its quality of life: its clean environment, recreational opportunities, and stimulating cultural scene . . . If the region is to continue to grow and develop, it must take full advantage of all of its assets. It also means that the assets that have made the economy what it is, such as its workforce capabilities and its quality of life, receive the reinvestment necessary to keep them strong.

The Austin case illustrates how far-sighted regions are recognizing that continued success in the high-technology economy will turn on the ability to deliver environmental quality, natural amenities, and the lifestyle desired by knowledge workers.

Talent and Amenities

In the creative economy, the ability to attract talent creates regional advantage. Contrast this with the old economy, where regional competition revolved around the competition for firms. The location decisions of firms drove regional economies, and the location decisions of people followed from the location of firms, who in turn based their decisions on natural resource endowments, transportation systems, and labor costs. The creative economy dramatically alters this calculus. Creative workers are both highly mobile and eagerly sought after by technology employers, and thus have the option of locating virtually anywhere they desire. At the same time, regional growth increasingly turns upon the ability to generate, attract, and maintain the talent base needed to create and grow technology-based companies.

Indeed, pioneering research by Robert Lucas and Edward Glaeser suggests that the key to regional competitiveness lies in the ability to attract high-skilled people, or human capital, and to generate ideas. Now, a whole generation of *new urban economists* and *new economic geographers* is concluding that *non-market* forces and interactions increasingly lie at the heart of regional economic development.

Another way of saying this is that sociological factors are as important—if not more important—than economic factors in generating and sustaining regional advantage in the creative economy.[13] These sociological factors revolve around creating the broad environment that is attractive to talent. In the creative economy, then, the *quality* of a region's lifestyle has as much to do with its success as its business cost structure, taxes, or physical location. How else can one explain the tremendous success of the highest cost locations—regions like Silicon Valley, the greater Boston area, Washington, D.C., and Seattle? A key dimension of regional advantage turns on the ability of a place to capture the imagination, dreams, and desires of young creative workers who are making location decisions.

The ability to attract talent is a key factor in regional competitiveness, according to several studies. For instance, a 1999 study by the Southern Technology Council examined the migration trends of recent high school and college graduates in science and engineering fields using data from the national Science Foundation.[14] Overall, the report found that the ability to *attract* talent was more important than the ability to retain it. This is an important point given that many regions are developing talent retention strategies to retain existing people or lure back those who have moved away. This chapter suggests that broader efforts to attract talent on a national scale are likely to be more efficacious in the long run.

The top states for talent retention were California, Texas, Massachusetts, Michigan, and several others. These states retained between 67 and 84 percent of their college graduates in science and engineering fields, and between 60 and 81 percent of their high school graduates in science and engineering fields. Leading high-technology states were consistently in the first and second quartiles on this measure.

The top states for talent attraction were New Jersey, Vermont, California, and Texas. New Jersey and Vermont attracted between one and more than two times their number of college graduates, while California and Texas attracted from 1.15 to more than 1.5 times the number of high school students they graduated. Again, leading high-technology states were consistently in the first or second quartile on this measure. The report notes that retaining high school graduates—that is sending them to high-quality colleges and universities in state—is an important step in retaining talent generally.

A region's ability to attract talent, though, depends in large part on its quality of place. To get a better handle on this relationship, we compared regions on the basis of their amenities and their ability to generate high-technology industry and attract talent. We did this for the benchmark regions following the same basic methodology used for the environment. The bottom line of the analysis is clear: Leading high-technology regions are also high amenity regions.

- Three high-technology regions—Boston, Washington, D.C., and Seattle—score highly in terms of overall amenities and high-technology development, being located in the far upper right corner of Figure 3.8. San Francisco, Denver, Atlanta, Oakland, San Diego, Raleigh, and Austin, as well as Philadelphia and Houston, also score well on this measure.

- Washington, D.C., San Francisco, and Boston score highly in terms of overall amenities and creative workers, occupying the far upper right-hand quadrant of Figure 3.9.
- San Jose, Dallas, Minneapolis, Seattle, Denver, and Atlanta also fare reasonably well on this measure.
- Even several older industrial regions such as Baltimore, Pittsburgh, and Cleveland rank highly in terms of amenities, but they have not generated high-technology growth. This suggests that the overall amenity packages of these regions may not be in sync with the demands of talent.

However, there is a considerable difference between the amenities of industrial and creative economies. The industrial economy emphasized *big ticket* amenities like professional sports, the fine arts (e.g., opera, classical music, and the theater), and cultural destinations (e.g., museums

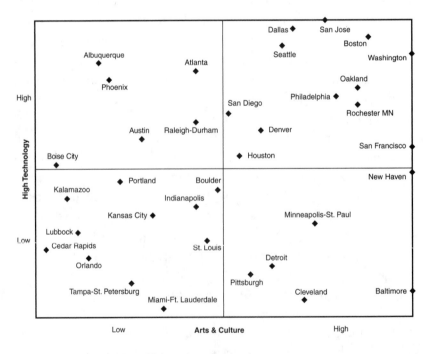

Source: www.milken-inst.org and www.pathfinder.com/money/bestplaces/

Figure 3.8 Arts and culture and high technology

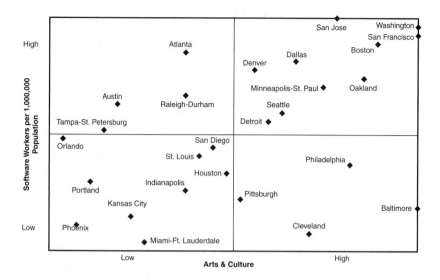

Figure 3.9 Arts and culture and software workers

and art exhibits). Creative economy amenities typically revolve around outdoor recreational activities and lifestyle amenities. While there is not much in the way of systematic and comparable data that allows one to examine these differences, we constructed a variety of measures to probe the differences between new and old economy amenities.

Amenities like symphonies, opera companies, museums, and art galleries are certainly desirable. But there is no clear relationship between arts and culture and either high-technology industries or the ability to attract creative workers.[15] A number of leading high-technology regions are also exceptionally endowed in terms of arts and culture. But other leading high-technology regions score rather poorly on this measure. Furthermore, several regions that rank low in terms of both creative workers and high-technology score relatively highly in terms of arts and culture. This leads to the conclusion that while arts and cultural amenities are helpful in attracting high-technology industries and creative workers, they alone are not enough, as other amenities come into play.

- San Jose, Boston, and Washington, D.C., for example, score highly in term of amenities and high-technology development, occupying the far upper right-hand quadrant of Figure 3.10, while Seattle and Dallas also score quite highly on this measure.
- Washington, D.C., Boston, and San Francisco top the list in terms of arts and culture and creative workers, occupying the far upper right-hand quadrant of Figure 3.11.
- San Jose, Dallas, Oakland, Denver, Seattle, Minneapolis, and surprisingly Detroit also score reasonably well on this measure.

A number of a regions that have been successful in generating high-technology and attracting talent—particularly Austin and Raleigh-Durham—score poorly in terms of arts and culture. And, ironically, several regions that rank relatively low in terms of high-technology industry and/or talent—such as Baltimore, Philadelphia, Pittsburgh, Detroit, and Cleveland—have among the highest rankings in terms of arts and culture.

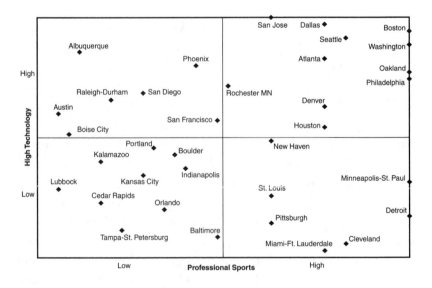

Source: www.milken-inst.org and www.pathfinder.com/money/bestplaces/

Figure 3.10 Professional sports and high technology

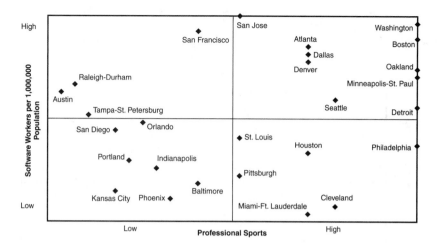

Source: County Business Patterns and www.pathfinder.com/money/bestplaces/

Figure 3.11 Professional sports and software workers

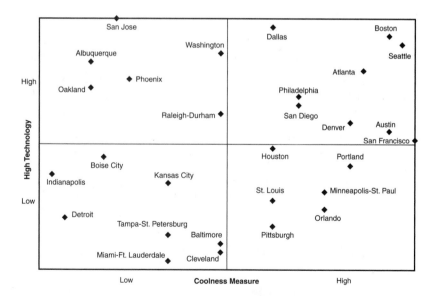

Source: www.milken-inst.org and "Boom Town USA," POV, December/January 1999, pp. 69–81

Figure 3.12 Coolness Index and high technology

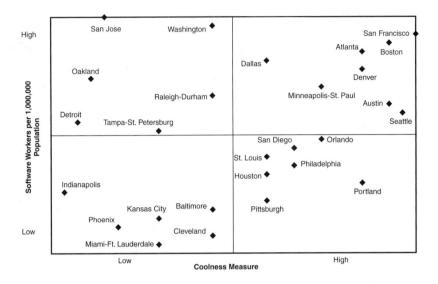

Figure 3.13 Coolness Index and software workers

Traditional arts and culture institutions are not the only poor indicators of high-technology industrial growth. For decades, cities have pursued major league sports franchises to put themselves on the map. But while professional sports are increasingly seen as a mechanism for achieving big league status and attracting talent, the data suggest that there is little relationship between them and high-technology or creative workers.[16] While a number of leading high-technology regions—Boston, Washington, D.C., Seattle, and Dallas—score highly in terms of professional sports, others score quite poorly (see Figures 3.14 and 3.15.) Indeed, many successful high-technology regions—notably Austin and Raleigh-Durham—have little or no professional sports presence at all.

Ironically, it is smaller, less prestigious venues that possess the amorphous quality of cool that seem to be more effective attractors of high-tech firms. *POV Magazine* published a Coolness Index to measure a region's appeal in terms of amenities like nightlife, bars, restaurants, and

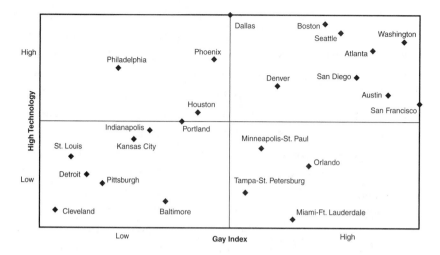

Source: www.milken-inst.org and Gates, et al, *Why Do Gay Men Live in San Francisco?* 1997

Figure 3.14 Gay Index and high technology

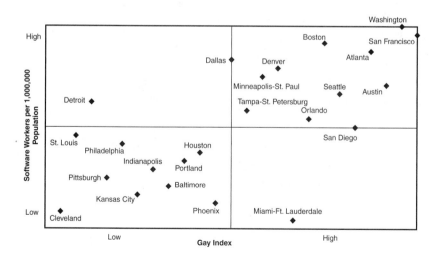

Source: County Business Patterns and Gates, et al, *Why Do Gay Men Live in San Francisco?* 1997

Figure 3.15 Gay Index and software workers

so on. There appears to be some relationship between this coolness measure, high-technology development, and talent. Leading high-technology regions like Boston, Seattle, Austin, and San Francisco score highly in terms of the coolness measure and high technology (Figure 3.16). The same regions also score highly in terms of the coolness measure and software workers (Figure 3.13). Atlanta, Denver, Minneapolis, and Dallas also score reasonably on these measures.

Finally, focus group evidence indicates that one of the most important amenities desired by young creative workers is a diverse cultural and demographic population. Gary Gates has researched the issue of local and regional diversity and has developed a proxy measure (the Gay Index) of regional diversity by measuring the concentration of gay households in Metropolitan Statistical Areas. This measure is a proxy for a region's openness and attractiveness to alternative lifestyles, a characteristic that was noted as a key element of diversity by creative workers in the focus groups. While far from a perfect measure of overall diversity, the Gay Index does provide a reasonable proxy for the kind of cultural and lifestyle diversity that young creative workers seem to desire. The data, shown in Figure 3.16, suggest a high degree of correlation

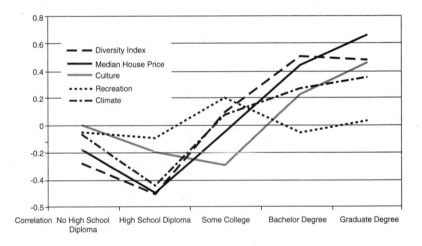

Source: Gates, Arora, Florida, and Kamlet, "Amenities and the Location of Knowledge Workers" (Carnegie Mellon University, H. John Heinz III School of Public Policy and Management, January 2000)

Figure 3.16 Correlation between education level, amenities, and diversity

between the Gay Index and a region's success in attracting high-technology businesses and talent. Leading high-technology regions—Washington, D.C., Boston, Seattle, Austin, and San Francisco—all score highly in terms of diversity, high technology, and talent. So, it would appear that successful high-technology regions are also regions that support or even promote demographic diversity.

Econometric research conducted by myself and a team of Carnegie Mellon researchers provides additional confirmation of the link between amenities and talent. It examined this issue across 115 industries in 67 Metropolitan Statistical Areas (MSAs) with populations over 500,000. It used multivariate regression analysis to examine the effect of amenities on employment in industries with different worker skill requirements or knowledge intensity. The research suggests that as an industry's need for high-skill or knowledge-intensive labor increases, it is more likely to employ workers in cities with high amenity levels.

The findings also indicate that high-skill and knowledge-intensive workers and the industries that employ them are more likely to locate in high-amenity areas, which tend to have higher costs of living. Figure 3.16 nicely illustrates this, graphing the statistical correlation between several measures of amenities and the percentage of the population with various levels of educational attainment or knowledge intensity. As this graph shows, there is a clear relationship between amenities and education, the correlation between amenities and talent rising sharply alongside educational level.[17] Furthermore, the correlation between amenities and knowledge intensity tends to be highly positive for talent (measured as the percentage of the population with bachelors and graduate degrees) and negative for others (measured as percentage of the population with high school degree or less).

Regions around the nation and the world are undertaking efforts to bolster and enhance their amenity offerings and quality of life. This is particularly true of rapidly growing high-technology centers, such as Seattle and Austin, that have both made amenities an increasingly important component of their economic growth strategies. Even before their high-tech booms, both regions developed amenity strategies early on and were recognized as highly desirable places to live before they became high-technology growth centers. They possessed thriving music scenes, a wealth of high-quality, casual restaurants, a commitment to preserving natural beauty, smart growth, and a solid focus on outdoor recreational amenities.

LIFESTYLE MATTERS—BURLINGTON, VERMONT

Burlington has used lifestyle as a lever for economic development. A smaller city on the banks of Lake Champlain, Burlington is becoming a growing center for knowledge workers and high-technology industry. The city ranked fifth in *POV* magazine's list of the top 75 boomtowns in America and fourth in *Utne Reader*'s list of America's Most Enlightened Cities.

Burlington has sought to combine economic development, environmental health, and outdoor amenities into a powerful package for generating sustainable economic advantage. The city has combined entrepreneurship, commitment to diversity, progressive and participatory civic culture, and commitment to the environmental and natural amenities to spur economic development. It has encouraged local business ownership and leveraged assets such as the University of Vermont and its proximity to Lake Champlain. The presence of the University of Vermont is an important part of its lifestyle mix and serves as an attraction for students, professionals, and entrepreneurs.

Burlington has actively worked to revitalize its waterfront along Lake Champlain and to make public transportation seamless and accessible to all residents. The city views entrepreneurship and progressive government as complementary, not contradictory. Burlington has emphasized natural amenities and outdoor recreation. While cities like Austin and Seattle are known for their music scenes and nightlife, Burlington boasts excellent skiing in the winter and boating, hiking, and cycling in the summer. It has been rated a top walking city by *Walking Magazine*, due in part to the city's commitment to maintaining and restoring historic sites. The city has tried to insure that all citizens can benefit from the waterfront area, adding a nine-mile bike path with a view of the Adirondack Mountains and, instead of a private yacht club, a community boathouse where anyone can rent sailboats.

The city was a pioneer in the development of a pedestrian mall near the University of Vermont. The pedestrian mall was created by closing a street between the university and the waterfront and working to attract high-end retail establishments to the location. In contrast to failed pedestrian malls in other cities, Burlington's mall has been successful, with a combination of upscale retailers like the Gap or Banana Republic and locally-owned establishments like used book stores and coffee shops. It also boasts a redeveloped waterfront, park space, beaches, and a wildlife refuge along a 6.5-mile walking and cycling path, which extends all the way around Lake Champlain. The city has long been at the forefront on recycling, green design, and sustainability. It converted an industrial zone into the Pine Street business incubator, which now provides office space for over 80 start-up companies.

With its commitment to natural amenities, youthful orientation, environmental quality, and quality of life, Burlington has become an increasingly attractive place for knowledge workers and a growing cadre of entrepreneurial high-technology enterprises. With a strong commitment to sustainable development, Burlington can continue to grow without losing the natural assets that have made it so attractive.

TECHNOLOGY, LIFESTYLE, AND AMENITIES IN AUSTIN

The city of Austin, Texas, is arguably the top U.S. high-technology success story of the past two decades. Building on the success of Dell Computers (founded in 1984), Austin has become one of the country's pre-eminent centers for computer and software development. Today, the city is home to over 1,750 high-technology companies (including companies such as IBM, Motorola, and Dell) employing over 110,000 people (or 20 percent of the city's total employment).

As a leading center of high-technology industry, Austin has a large pool of locally educated knowledge workers (the University of Texas has a total enrollment of over 48,000 students), a wide range of recreational opportunities, and a commitment to a high quality of life. The city's workforce is well educated; over 32 percent of Austin's adults have the equivalent of a bachelor's degree, and over 11 percent have the equivalent of a graduate degree (with another 10 percent enrolled in graduate study).

Austin exemplifies a city that has made the environment and recreational amenities one of the cornerstones of its economic development. Before 1983, when Microelectronics and Computer Technology Corporation (MCC) decided to locate there, Austin was known for its thriving music scene (e.g., Austin City Limits) and laid-back, outdoor-oriented lifestyle. The city is regularly recognized as being among the top cities in the country for live music and alternative film, and offers a diverse array of night-life options combined with outdoor activities like rock climbing, bow hunting, and mountain biking. The city constantly ranks among the top cities in the country in economic, recreational, and environmental listings. It has been ranked in the top ten in such lists as *Forbes's* best cities for business (#1), *Fortune's* high technology ranking (#2), *POV* magazine's boomtown rankings (#2), *Walking* magazine's best large walking towns (#5), and *Bicycling* magazine's top cycling cities (#6).

Austin's two-pronged approach to economic development began in 1984, when the city attempted to capitalize on the presence of government-based research consortiums like MCC and Sematech to build a technology-based economic cluster in the region. The city focused primarily on leveraging its university roots and a small existing base of technology manufacturing to develop a core of R&D centers. The combination of public and private research, high technology manufacturing, and commercial R&D led to the formation of a technology-based economy, focused primarily on personal computers, software, and electronics. An entrepreneurial atmosphere combined with available venture capital has led to a rapidly growing number of technology start-ups.

Austin also has focused its effort on lifestyle and quality of life issues. The city has cultivated its recreational and cultural amenities in an attempt to attract and retain high-quality talent. This is an ongoing process, and one of Austin's priorities in the coming years is to further increase the number of cultural and recreational outlets in the city. Additionally, Austin's environmental record has been stellar. In 1995, Austin did not exceed any federal air quality standard, and the city does not have a single Superfund cleanup site.

If Austin has a shortcoming, it may be that it has grown too fast. Residents have begun to complain that the city suffers from urban sprawl and has lost some of its character among new suburbs. The cost of living has risen dramatically, with home prices as much as doubling (though still much lower than in larger cities like New York or San Francisco). Austin has begun to take steps to address these problems by implementing more effective land use programs and zoning codes, and by looking at ways to reuse abandoned downtown land. The city has begun to identify geographic clusters of various industries in order to better map out future transportation needs and solutions. It has attempted to bring planning agencies together in a planning summit, to allow for more seamless sharing of ideas. The city is committed to smart growth and sustainable development as a key component of its regional economic development agenda.

Austin's success reflects its commitment to both high-technology industry and the lifestyle amenities required to attract and to retain talent in the new economy.

More recently, both regions have undertaken strategic efforts to improve the quality of life for the area where creative workers reside. That is, they have focused considerable energy and resources on improving and maintaining a high quality of life in the areas surrounding major university campuses as well as emphasizing more traditional downtown revitalization.

This focus on lifestyle and quality of life around major universities has become typical of most leading high technology regions. The major centers of high technology in areas like the Silicon Valley, the Route 128 area, or Seattle are not in the established downtowns of San Francisco, Boston, or Seattle. Rather, fledgling high-technology enterprises are typically incubated in and around the districts surrounding major university campuses and later move to technology campuses in more suburban locations as they expand.

For instance, there have been major investments in renovating and refurbishing the Kendall Square area around MIT, which was once run-down and blighted. Now, renovated factory and warehouse districts are home startup companies, venture capital funds, restaurants, microbreweries, cafes, and hotels. Downtown Palo Alto, bordering Stanford University, functions as a hub for activities and amenities with upscale shops, restaurants, cafes, and hotels, as well as offices for startup companies, venture capitalists, and high-echnology service providers. University districts like these provide visual cues that a region is "with it," occupies a place in the creative economy, is youth-friendly, and values the technological and entrepreneurial contribution associated with its major universities. Such areas perform a critical function as a magnet for retaining and attracting talent and as places young creative workers want to live and work.

What Does Talent Want?

As we have already seen, talent is a key element of regional competitiveness in the creative economy. So it is vitally important to better understand what talented people look for in a place to live and work. A 1998 KPMG survey of more than 1200 high-technology workers examined the factors associated with the attractiveness of a new job. It found that *community quality of life* was the second most important factor—just below salary—and more important than benefits, stock options, or company stability.[18]

- *Salary:* for every percentage increase in salary, the likelihood of attracting a person to a position increases by one percent.
- *Quality of life in the community:* increases the attractiveness of a job by 33 percent.
- *Proximity to family and friends:* increases the attractiveness of a job by 19 percent.
- *Benefits:* increase the attractiveness of a job by 17 percent.
- *Stock options:* increase the attractiveness of a job by 14 percent.
- *Established company:* a job with an established company increases in attractiveness by seven percent.

To get more detailed information on how creative workers choose places to live and work, we conducted a series of focus group studies in Pittsburgh, a town which houses a leading university in high technology studies, Carnegie Mellon University. The focus groups examined the factors associated with how and why young people in technology-based industries choose places to live and work. Participants included young creative workers who were either in the process of making, or had already made, their decisions about where to locate. They were asked a wide range of questions about their preferred cities and the reasons behind those choices. The groups were broken down into four segments: college juniors and seniors in technology-based fields, juniors and seniors in management or related fields, graduate students in all fields, and young professionals who had already entered the workforce. Focus group participants came from a wide array of places, including U.S. cities of varying sizes and foreign countries in Europe, South America, and Asia. There was considerable diversity across racial, ethnic, and gender lines. The undergraduate participants came from a more varied set of locations and were more diverse by ethnicity and gender. The young professionals were more homogenous. That is, they were more likely to be white males (which may stem from the fact that they had chosen Pittsburgh as a place to live and work).

The findings from these focus groups supplement the results of the statistical research and case studies, enabling us to zero in more precisely on the factors that affect the location choices of creative workers. First off, amenities clearly matter in the location choices of young creative workers. The focus group participants placed a high value on amenities and the environment in their choices of where to live and work. The focus group participants essentially *balanced economic opportunity and lifestyle* in selecting a place to live. They were not simply looking for a job—but a place where they could advance their career by moving among jobs, and that had a creative economy lifestyle. In fact, to some degree, the findings of the focus group research show that creative workers in high-technology fields place more emphasis on lifestyle factors, such as the environmental and recreational quality, of a region than on its job market when choosing where to live. The participants defined amenities to include:

- Large numbers of visibly active young people
- Easy access to a wide range of outdoor activities

- A vibrant music and performance scene with a wide range of live-music opportunities
- A wide range of night-life experiences, including many options without alcohol
- A clean, healthy environment and commitment to preserving natural resources for enjoyment and recreation
- A lifestyle that is youth-friendly and supportive of diversity

Indeed, many participants spoke of wanting to know that a particular amenity is around, almost as an external symbol of a region's vibrancy, even though they personally might not make use of that amenity.

This preference for high-amenity places is related to the nature of knowledge-work careers. Jobs in high-technology fields are stressful and require long working hours. Lifestyle amenities are seen as sources of stress relief. Young creative workers say that long working hours give them little time to enjoy themselves, so that when they do something *it has to be good.* Also, jobs and careers in high-technology fields are unstable and characterized by frequent turnover. Creative workers see their career as a portfolio of opportunities and experiences. According to the U.S. Labor Department, the median job tenure for workers ages 25 to 34 is just 2.7 years: and, by age 32, the average worker has had nine full- or part-time jobs. The old saying in Silicon Valley, where job-hopping is a well-established norm, quips: "You can change jobs without changing your parking lot." Given the reality of work and careers in the creative economy, focus group participants reported that they choose cities that both offer a robust array of job opportunities and are also a high-quality places to live. A high-amenity city that is a nice place to live provides a level of permanence that a job does not.

But the amenities these creative workers desire differ from traditional amenities. The amenity package of the industrial economy tended to focus on cultural amenities (the symphony, opera, theater, ballet, etc.) and on big-ticket items like national chain restaurants, nightspots, and major league sports venues. There is mounting evidence that, while still important, these types of amenities are taking a backseat to more casual, open, inclusive, and participative activities. Focus group participants expressed a preference for a diverse range of such activities, including outdoor amenities (e.g., rowing, cycling, and rock climbing) and other lifestyle activities (e.g., vibrant music scene, outdoor restaurants, organic supermarkets, and juice bars). They also preferred a wider range of nightlife activities not revolving exclusively around bars and drinking. Participants were looking for a wide range of experiences that are diverse, open, and inclusive of other young people, and drew a sharp distinction between these sorts of activities and more expensive and exclusive amenities like the symphony or even professional sports.

Accessibility is a major concern. Participants expressed a strong preference for regions where amenities and activities are easy to get to and available on a just-in-time basis, with easy access on foot, bicycle, or via public transportation. Many of the younger creative workers did not have cars and wanted to locate in regions where they did not need one. Furthermore, focus group participants expressed a preference for amenities that blend seamlessly with work. In other words, creative workers working long hours need to be able to access amenities almost instantly on demand, whether on their lunch break or immediately following the workday.

Young creative workers also expressed a desire to learn more about the city and region. They universally preferred mass transportation—subway or light rail—as a means for connecting to the broader region, and saw it as crucial in selecting a place to live and work. The mobility and connectivity provided by a subway or light rail system was noted as a key factor in the attractiveness of regions such as Boston, Washington, D.C., New York City, and Chicago. For a number of reasons, the bus system was not seen as providing that sort of connectivity.

Focus groups indicated both the importance of water-based activities like sailing, kayaking, and rowing, as well as the importance of access to the water for outings or nightlife. In fact, water seems to be a common theme among high-amenity regions. Several of the most successful high-technology cities are located on or near bodies of water and have utilized those bodies strategically to enhance both the local environment and the opportunity for recreation and transportation (see Boxes 3.4 and 3.5, Amenities and High Technology: Austin and Seattle).

Finally, focus group respondents noted the importance of diversity and the attractiveness of regions that reflect, and are supportive of, diversity. Typically, creative workers in technology-based industries come from diverse ethnic and racial backgrounds and desire places that reflect that diversity. They also look for environments where they can easily fit in. Creative economy amenities—lifestyle, outdoor, and recreational amenities—are not just important in and of themselves, but provide signals or visual cues of a diverse, supportive, youth-friendly environment. Focus group participants expressed a preference for places where they can readily plug in and develop a support structure of colleagues and friends. This is particularly important to recognize as many of these young people are relocating without the support structure of friends and family.

Summary

To gain competitive advantage, regions need to create mechanisms for harnessing the knowledge and ideas of all citizens at the neighborhood, local, and regional levels for improving their quality of place.

This kind of strategy would be relatively inexpensive, as it involves marshalling resources (parks, rivers, etc.) that are already in place. It is also strongly place-based and, as such, confers direct benefits on broad segments of the local population and industry, in contrast to conferring large subsidies to non-residents or outside industry.

Quality of place is a critical piece of the total package that enables regions to attract talent. This—along with good, challenging, high-reward jobs—is a large part of the reasons why some regions are winning the competition for talent. Jobs, then, are a necessary, but insufficient, condition in this battle for talent. It is quality of place that completes the picture.

4
THE ECONOMIC GEOGRAPHY OF TALENT

"What is important for growth is integration not into an economy with a large number of people, but rather into one with a large amount of human capital."
—*Paul Romer*[1]

The distribution of talent, or human capital, is an important factor in economic geography. Indeed, it determines why some cities succeed and others decline. Geographers have paid considerable attention to the geography of labor, suggesting that key factors in the location decisions of firms include labor costs and labor quality. Jane Jacobs long ago called attention to the role of cities in attracting and mobilizing talented and creative people.[2] Edwin Ullman also recognized the role of talent or human capital in his classic work on regional development and the geography of concentration.[3] Robert Lucas has argued that the driving force behind the growth and development of cities and regions is the productivity gains associated with the clustering of talented people or human capital.[4]

There has been less research on the factors that attract talent and shape its economic geography. For the most part, geographers and social scientists have viewed the economic geography of talent as a function of employment opportunities and financial incentives. A growing stream of research suggests that amenities, entertainment, and lifestyle considerations are important elements of the ability of cities to attract both firms and people.[5]

This chapter examines the economic geography of talent, focusing in particular on the factors that attract human capital or talent. As we shall see, this economic geography is associated with diversity or openness— what I refer to as *low barriers to entry for human capital*. I also explore the effect of the economic geography of talent on high-technology industry and regional incomes.

Both qualitative and quantitative research on the factors associated with the economic geography of talent and its effects on high-technology industry location and regional income shed light on these trends. As a proxy for human capital, I measured talent as the percentage of the population with a bachelor's degree and then used two supplementary measures: the percentage of total employment that includes scientists and engineers, and similarly the percentage of professional and technical workers. As a proxy for diversity, I used the Gay Index, based on the proportion of coupled gay households in a region's population. Another measure, the Coolness Index, accounts for cultural and night-life amenities.

The findings tell us much about both the factors associated with the economic geography of talent and the effects of that geography on regional development. The economic geography of talent is highly concentrated at the regional level. Talent is associated with the diversity index, confirming that talent is attracted to places with low-entry barriers for human capital. And while certainly important to city growth, climate, recreational, and cultural amenities turn out to be less important inducements to talented workers than diversity. Furthermore, talent is strongly associated with high-technology industry location. From this, talent and high-technology industry work independently and together to generate higher regional incomes. In short, talent is a key intermediate variable in attracting high-technology industries and generating higher regional incomes.

Concepts and Theory[6]

Talent and Regional Growth

Jacobs called attention to the central role played by people in the generation and organization of economic activity in cities.[7] In her view, cities play a crucial role in economic development, through the generation and mobilization of new knowledge. The scale of cities and their diversity of inhabitants creates the interactions that generate new ideas. In other words, the diversity of economic actors within cities and their high level of interaction promote the creation and development of new products and new technology. Ullman also noted the role played by human capital or talent in the process of regional development and the geography of concentration.[8] Ake Andersson and Pierre Desroshers noted that the ability to incubate and nurture creativity and to attract creative people is a central factor in regional development.[9] The *new growth theory* associated with Romer formally highlights the connection between knowledge, human capital, and economic growth.[10] Building upon these insights, Lucas essentially argued that cities function to collect and organize human capital, giving rise to strong external economies, which he refers to as external human capital.[11] He concluded that these economies increase productivity and spur urban growth.

Empirical studies support the human capital-regional growth connection. Eaton and Eckstein and Black and Henderson have suggested that, given spillovers in the accumulation of human capital, workers are more productive when they locate around others with high levels of human capital.[12] Other empirical studies have found that human capital is strongly associated with urban and regional growth. Rauch found that both wages and housing rents were higher in cities with higher average education levels.[13] Edward Glaeser and his collaborators found a strong relationship between human capital and city growth,[14] noting that cities that begin with more educated populations exhibit higher rates of population growth as time goes on. Simon and Nardinelli examined the connection between human capital and city growth in the United States and Great Britain, finding that the level of human capital in 1880 predicted city growth in subsequent decades.[15] Glaeser found that access to common pools of labor or talent is what underpins the tendency of firms to cluster together in regional agglomerations, rather than interfirm linkages.[16] Curtis Simon and Spencer Glendon independently identified strong relationships between the average level of human capital and regional employment growth over a considerable time frame.[17] I found a positive relationship between technological creativity (measured as regional innovation and high-technology industry) and cultural creativity (measured by a *Bohemian Index*—that is, the regional share of artists, musicians, and cultural producers). Gary Gates and I pinpointed a positive relationship between regional concentrations of high-technology industry and several measures of diversity, including the percent of the population that is foreign-born, the percent that is gay, and a composite diversity measure (see Chapter 6).

The Location of Talent

The literature suggests that places attract human capital or talent through two interrelated mechanisms. The traditional view offered by economists is that places attract people by matching them to jobs and economic opportunity. More recent research suggests that places attract people by providing a range of lifestyle amenities.[18] This is particularly true of highly educated, high-human capital individuals who possess resources, are economically mobile, and can exercise considerable choice in their location. Richard Lloyd and Terry Clark argue that amenities are a key component of modern cities, referring to this lifestyle-oriented city as an "Entertainment Machine."[19] Joel Kotkin argues that high-technology industries and workers are attracted to a range of lifestyle amenities.[20] Glaeser and others found a significant relationship between amenities and city growth.[21] They suggest not only that high human capital workers increase productivity, but that high human capital areas are pleasant places to live, concluding that "If cities are to remain strong, they must attract workers on the basis of quality of life as well as on the basis of higher wages." In a review of the literature, Glaeser notes that cities attract people as well as firms through the interplay of both market and nonmarket forces at work within them.[22]

The Role of Diversity and Tolerance

Diversity plays a central and crucial role in attracting talent—i.e., human capital. Urban and regional economists have long argued that diversity is important to regional economic performance. In the main, the term *diversity* is used to refer to the diversity of firms or regional industrial structures. In a major review of the field, John Quigley suggests that regional economies benefit from the location of a diverse set of firms and industries.[23]

The argument advanced here is different. It suggests that diversity plays a key role in the attraction and retention of the kinds of talent required to support high-technology industry and generate regional growth. Jacobs called attention to the role of diversity and immigration in powering innovation and city growth.[24] Following Jacobs, Pierre Desroshers notes the relationships between diversity, creativity, and regional innovation.[25] Pascal Zachary argues that openness to immigration is a key factor in innovation and economic growth.[26] He notes that the United States' competitiveness in high-technology fields is directly linked to its openness to outsiders, while the relative stagnation of Japan and Germany is tied to *closedness* and relative homogeneity. In an empirical study of Silicon Valley, Annalee Saxenian found that roughly one-quarter of new business formations had a Chinese- or Indian-born founder and that roughly one-third of the region's scientists and engineers were foreign-born.[27]

To reiterate, diversity—or low entry barriers for talent—increase a region's ability to compete for talent. At any given time, regions, like firms, compete with one another for talent. To support high-technology industries or a broad range of economic activity in general, regions compete for a variety of talent across a wide variety of fields and disciplines. Regions that are open to diversity are thus able to attract a wider range of talent by nationality, race, ethnicity, and sexual orientation than are those that remain relatively closed. And regions that are open and possess low barriers to entry for human capital gain distinct economic advantage in the competition for talent or human capital and, in turn, in their ability to generate and attract high-technology industries and increase their incomes. Figure 4.1 outlines the structure of these relationships.

Research and Methods

An empirical analysis of the economic geography of talent, the factors that attract talent, and talent's effects on high-technology industry location and growth as well as regional income can tell us much about the process. The Pittsburgh-based focus groups of talented knowledge workers discussed in the previous chapter bear the thesis out.[28] We probed respondents who were in the process of making location decisions or had recently made such decisions about the key factors that mattered to them in the choice of particular locations. We also interviewed respondents about the key economic, cultural, and lifestyle factors that affected their choices of particular locations in which to live and work. Four structured studies were conducted involving graduating undergraduate students in technical fields, graduating undergraduate students in nontechnical fields, graduating graduate students in business and technical fields, and professionals who had recently made location decisions.[29] Subsequent field research and personal interviews were conducted with individuals making location decisions in various cities and regions across the United States. The qualitative research was exploratory in nature and designed to shed light on and help structure the quantitative research, which was confirmatory in nature and approach.

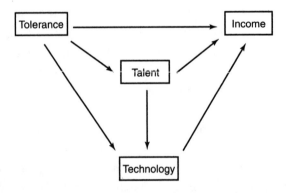

Figure 4.1 Structure of a region's relationships: Technology, Talent, and Tolerance

Data, Variables, and Methods

Statistical analysis examined the geography of talent, the factors associated with that observed geography, and the effect of talent on the characteristics of regional economies. It included descriptive statistics, correlation or bivariate analysis, multivariate regression analysis, and path analysis. Measures used include a Talent Index, amenity measures, a Coolness Index, a Diversity Index, a medium home value measure, a Tech-Pole index, and a regional income index. Table 4.1 provides descriptive statistics for the various measures used in this research.

The Talent Index is a measure of highly educated people, defined as those with a bachelor's degree and above. This index is normalized on a percentage basis or per thousand people and based on the *1990 Decennial Census Public Use Microdata Sample.* Two additional measures of talent are also used: professional and technical workers, and scientists and engineers. Both of these are normalized on a percentage basis or per thousand people and based on the *1990 Decennial Census Public Use Microdata Sample.*

I used several measures of amenities as well. These are based on traditional indicators of climatic, cultural, and recreational amenities adapted from the 1989 *Places Rated Almanac.*[30]

The Coolness Index is a measure adapted from the so-called *coolness factor* used by *POV Magazine* (December-January 1999.) The measure is

Table 4.1 Descriptive Statistics

VARIABLE	OBS	MEAN	STD DEV	MIN	MAX
Diversity	50	1.32	0.87	0.19	5.39
High Tech	50	1.40	1.88	0.06	8.24
Scientists & Engineers	50	15.77	5.62	6.33	30.93
Professional & Technical	50	286.84	30.27	235.75	356.18
Talent	50	0.24	0.05	0.14	0.42
Coolness	43	6.35	1.51	1.00	10.00
Median House Value	48	84.65	30.60	51.39	186.20
Cultural Amenity	50	1804.76	1458.98	482.00	9375.56
Recreational Amenity	50	2275.82	727.94	933.00	4390.00
Climate	50	579.91	116.79	293.00	903.00
Per Capita Income	50	24350.10	3264.02	19412.92	34751.28
Per Capita Income Change	50	2881.09	982.89	297.38	4682.39

based on the percentage of population ages 22 to 29 (with points added for diversity), nightlife (number of bars, nightclubs, and the like per capita) and culture (number of art galleries and museums per capita).

The Diversity Index, or Gay Index, is a measure of the fraction of the population that is gay.[31] The reason it is a good proxy is that the gay population is a segment of the population that has long faced discrimination and ostracism. The presence of a relatively large gay population thus functions as a signal indicator of a region that is open to various other groups. The Gay Index is based on data from the 1990 Decennial Census (five percent sample), identifying households in which a householder and an unmarried partner were both of the same sex (in this case, male). Approximately 0.01 percent of the population was composed of gay, coupled men. The index is basically a location quotient that measures the number of gay households compared to the national population of gay households divided by the population in the city compared to the total national population.

A median house-value measure allowed for an examination of the effects of talent on housing costs. Because of Rosen, researchers have argued that amenities are at least partially capitalized in land rents.[32] This measure is also adapted from the 1990 Decennial Census.

The analysis also uses the Milken Institute's *Tech-Pole Index*, which examines the effect of talent on the location of high-technology industry. The index is a composite measure based on the percent of national high-technology real output multiplied by the high-technology real-output location quotient for each metropolitan statistical area (MSA.)[33]

Finally, I use a measure to examine the effect of talent on regional income. Two measures of income are used: per capita income level and absolute income change. Income level is for 1997, and income change covers the period from 1991 to 1997. These data are from the Bureau of Economic Analysis.

Statistical and Econometric Analysis

Both bivariate and multivariate analyses were conducted to examine the factors associated with the economic geography of talent and the effect of that geography (controlling for other factors) on high-technology industry location and regional income. Path analysis is used to better understand the structure of relationships among these variables. We used path analysis to discern the path of relationships in a model with multiple competing paths of causality. It should be pointed out that path analysis does not prove the direction of causality, but can provide support for a certain path of causality.

The analysis is based on the 50 largest metropolitan regions, each with populations of 700,000 and above. For most regions, the MSA is employed as the unit of analysis. MSAs that are part of a consolidated metropolitan statistical area (CMSA) are combined into their CMSA as a single unit of analysis. MSA-level variables are weighted by their proportion of the CMSA and then summed at the CMSA level. The CMSA is used as the unit of analysis for the five largest regions: San Francisco, Los Angeles, Miami-Fort Lauderdale, New York, and Dallas-Fort Worth.

From the various research tools, we can construct a good descriptive overview of the economic geography of talent in America. We can also get at the factors that attract talent and shape that geography. Finally, the tools allow us to clearly see the effect of talent on high-technology location and regional incomes.

The Economic Geography of Talent

The economic geography of talent is uneven, as Figure 4.2 shows. Roughly 42 percent of the population of the top-ranked region, Washington, D.C., has a bachelor's degree or above. Washington, D.C., is followed by Boston, San Francisco, Austin, Atlanta, and Seattle respectively, and in all of these regions, more than 30 percent of the population holds a bachelor's degree or above. However, in more than 30 of the top 50 regions, less than 25 percent of the population has a bachelor's degree or above. Just 14 percent of the population of the region ranked 50th, Las Vegas, has a bachelor's degree or above. Similar patterns hold for scientists and engineers and professional and technical workers. Table 4.2 presents the results of a correlation analysis. Figure 4.3 shows maps for cultural amenities, the Coolness Index, and Diversity or Gay Index.

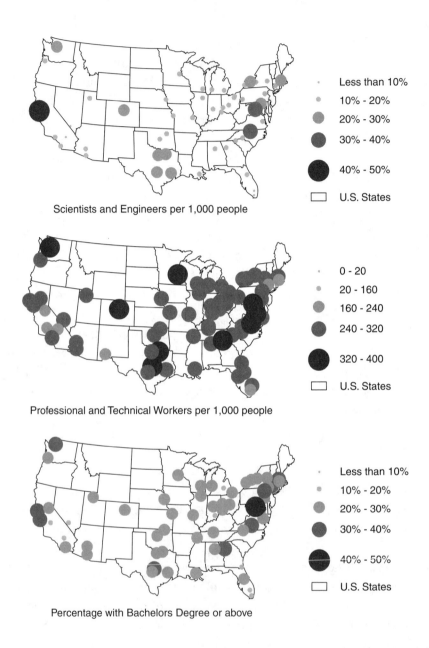

Scientists and Engineers per 1,000 people

Professional and Technical Workers per 1,000 people

Percentage with Bachelors Degree or above

Source: 1990 Decennial census, Public Use Microdata Sample (1 and 5 percent sample)

Figure 4.2 Mapping talent

Table 4.2 Correlation Analysis

	TALENT	DIVERSITY	HIGH TECH	CULTURAL AMENITIES	RECREATIONAL AMENITIES	CLIMATE	COOLNESS	MEDIAN HOUSE VALUE	PER CAPITA INCOME	PER CAPITA INCOME CHANGE
Talent	1.000									
Diversity	.7181***	1.000								
High Tech	.723***	.768***	1.000							
Cultural Amenities	.430***	.289**	.493***	1.000						
Recreational Amenities	−.048	.157	.159	.249*	1.000					
Climate	.220	.447***	.464***	.205	.291**	1.000				
Coolness	.469***	.377**	.429***	.569***	.246	.146	1.000			
Median House Value	.538***	.446**	.506***	.445***	.398***	.432***	.355**	1.000		
Per Capita Income	.588***	.498***	.601***	.521***	.096	.217	.417***	.380**	1.000	
Absolute Per Capita Income Change	.292**	.199	.321**	.182	−.187	−.119	.237	−.126	.517***	1.000

Note
*significant at 0.1
**significant at 0.05
***significant at 0.01

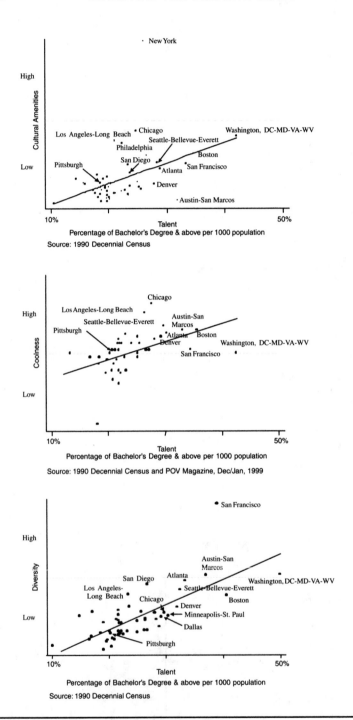

Figure 4.3 Amenities, diversity, and talent

Amenities

The results of the correlation analysis support what the previous chapter argued—that talented individuals appear to be attracted more by cultural amenities than by recreational amenities or climate (although the latter are not unimportant). The correlation coefficient for the basic Talent Index and cultural amenities is positive and significant (0.429, see Table 4.2). The same is true for professional and technical workers, but not for scientists and engineers, where the correlation coefficient is negative and insignificant. These relationships are in line with the findings of the interview and focus groups, which indicate that high human capital individuals exhibit a strong preference for cultural amenities. The correlations between talent and measures for both recreational amenities and climate are weak and mixed.

It is important to interpret these results with the following caveat in mind. The participants in the focus groups and interviews drew a sharp distinction between active outdoor recreation and spectator sports, such as professional baseball and football. The focus groups and interviews clearly indicate that talented individuals are attracted to places with high levels of active outdoor recreation. Here, it is important to note that the recreation measure is biased toward spectator sports. Because no reliable measures for such active outdoor recreation could be identified for the sample MSAs, the statistical research is unable to address the direct effect of active outdoor recreation.

Coolness

The correlation coefficient between the coolness measure and the Talent Index is 0.469. This finding is in line with the interview and focus group results, which indicate that highly educated, talented people—particularly younger workers who are active and those in knowledge-industry labor markets—are attracted to energetic and vibrant places. The focus group and interview subjects strongly emphasized the importance of visual and audio cues such as outdoor dining, active outdoor recreation, a thriving music scene, active nightlife, and bustling street scene as important attractants.

Median House Value

Median house value is positively associated with talent, the correlation being 0.538. The focus groups and interviews suggest that high human capital individuals are willing to pay more for higher levels of lifestyle and amenities. Indeed, median house value is correlated with coolness (0.355), the Diversity Index (0.446), and the cultural amenities (0.445). This stands in some contrast to conventional wisdom on the subject, which suggests that lower costs of living (reflected in lower median house values) may comprise an advantage in attracting talent.

Diversity

Talent is strongly associated with the Diversity Index. The correlation coefficient is 0.718, making it the highest correlation coefficient among this group of measures. This is also reflected in the scatter plot for talent and diversity. These results reflect the findings of the focus groups and interviews, which found that talented people are attracted to locations that have a high degree of demographic diversity and are distinguished by a high degree of openness and relatively low barriers to entry.

Multivariate Analysis

Multivariate regressions were used to further probe the factors associated with the economic geography of talent. Several models were run to gauge the effects of amenity measures (climate, culture, and recreation), coolness, and diversity on the location of talent. The results of the various models suggest a robust relationship (see Table 4.3).[34]

The most consistent finding is for diversity. The coefficient for the Diversity Index is consistently positive and highly significant in all permutations of the model.[35] These include both basic models and more complex ones where it is included alongside an array of other variables. This suggests that diversity (measured by the Gay Index) is strongly associated with the location of talent. The interviews and focus group findings are in line with this result. The focus groups and interview participants report that diversity is particularly important in the location decisions of high-human capital individuals.

The coolness measure is also associated with the location of talent. While it sometimes has significance in models where it is run alongside the diversity index, it is typically significant in models that do not include that index. The focus group and interview findings also suggest that high-human capital individuals, particularly younger ones, are drawn to places with vibrant music scenes, street-level culture, active nightlife, and other signifiers of "coolness."

The results for the amenity measures suggest that these cultural factors are not associated with the location of talent. The coefficients for cultural amenities are positive but never significant. The coefficients for climate are typically negative and are significant in only one permutation of the model.[36] The coefficients for recreational amenities are negative and significant. These findings suggest that talent is not necessarily drawn to warmer climates, greater recreational amenities, or cultural amenities. This can be attributed in part to the weaknesses of existing measures of amenities. For example, available measures of culture and recreation take into account only certain types of amenities. Yet the interview and focus group findings at least suggest that talented people are drawn to cultural and recreational amenities that are more broad based, open, and participative, such as active outdoor recreation or a vibrant music scene, which these measures do not reflect.

For the focus group members, these nonmarket or lifestyle factors also work in concert with economic opportunity in shaping the economic geography of talent. Clearly, people need to make a living and thus require gainful employment. Furthermore, the field research results indicate that high-human capital people have many employment options and change jobs relatively frequently, and thus they strongly favor locations that possess thick labor markets. Hence, high-paying, challenging employment is a necessary but insufficient condition to attract talent. Because high-human capital individuals are mobile and have many options, all of these conditions—particularly diversity— must be in place to attract them.

Talent and High-Technology Industry

I now turn to the relationship between talent and high-technology industry. A number of trends are readily apparent. Talent is quite closely

Table 4.3 Regression Model Findings: Talent and Quality of Place

Dependent Variable: Talent

VARIABLES	Model 1		Model 2		Model 3		Model 4	
	COEFFICIENT	P-VALUE	COEFFICIENT	P-VALUE	COEFFICIENT	P-VALUE	COEFFICIENT	P-VALUE
Diversity	0.0329	0.000***	0.0219	0.009***	0.0241	0.006***	0.021	0.007***
High Tech			0.0107	0.006***	0.0097	0.027**	0.0093	0.019**
Coolness Score	0.0049	0.196			0.0049	0.224	0.0044	0.211
Median House Value	0.0006	0.002***					0.0005	0.004***
Cultural Amenities	4.7400E-06	0.197			3.9900E-06	0.319	2.1E-06	0.552
Recreational Amenities	−2.3000E-05	0.002***			−1.4400E-05	0.047*	−2E-05	0.003***
Climate	−7.3100E-05	0.098*			−5.2600E-05	0.250	−9E-05	0.030**
R-square	0.7499	0.5875	0.7067	0.7878	0.6578		0.7442	
Adjusted R-square	0.7070		0.5700					
# of Observation	42		50		43		42	

Note

* significant at 0.10

** significant at 0.05

***significant at 0.01

correlated with high-technology industry, as measured by the Tech-Pole Index—a coefficient of 0.723 (see Table 4.2). High-technology industry is positively correlated with cultural amenities (0.493), climate (0.464), coolness (0.429), and median house value (0.506), but not with recreational amenities. But high-technology industry is even more closely correlated with the Diversity Index—a correlation coefficient of 0.768. Figure 4.4 provides scatter plots of high-technology industry and talent, and high-technology industry and diversity.

Multivariate regressions and path analysis also indicate considerably tight relationships between talent, diversity, and high-technology industry (see Table 4.4).[37] High-technology industry is associated with talent and diversity in virtually all permutations of the model. In the basic structure of the model, where talent and diversity are included as the only independent variables, both are positive and significant.[38] Interestingly, while high-technology industry is associated with diversity and talent, it does not appear to be associated with amenity variables or coolness. The coefficients for these variables are insignificant in most permutations of the model.

The results of the field research support these statistical findings. The interviews suggest that the availability of talent is an increasingly important location factor for these firms. They indicate that firms in knowledge-based industries are less concerned with traditional factors, such as land costs, labor costs, tax rates, or government incentives. Such firms report that they orient their location decisions to attract and retain talent. Places with large available talent pools reduce the costs associated with search and recruitment of talent. This is particularly important in highly competitive and highly innovative industries where speed to market is a critical success factor.

Path Analysis

Path analysis was used to further explore the path of causality among these variables. Figure 4.5 provides a schematic depiction of the key variables in the path analysis. A number of paths are of note.[39] First, talent is strongly associated with high-technology industry. Second, diversity is associated both with talent and high-technology industry. Diversity also works indirectly on high-technology industry via its

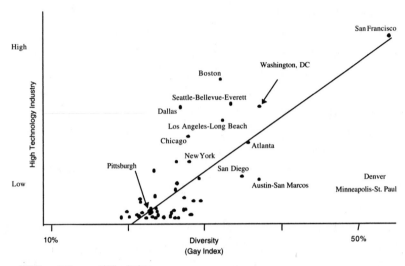

Source: 1990 Decennial Census and Milken Institute

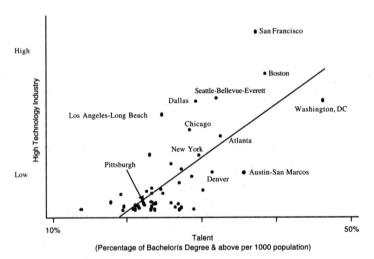

Source: 1990 Decennial Census and MilkenInstitute

Figure 4.4 High technology, talent, and diversity

Table 4.4 Regression Model Findings: Talent and High-Technology Industry

Dependent Variable: High Tech Industry

	Model 1		Model 2		Model 3		Model 4	
VARIABLES	COEFFICIENT	P-VALUE	COEFFICIENT	P-VALUE	COEFFICIENT	P-VALUE	COEFFICIENT	P-VALUE
Diversity	1.1070	0.000***	0.857	0.009***	1.0816	0.000***	1.3074	0.000***
Talent	13.8415	0.006***	13.2809	0.027**	11.7028	0.028**		
Coolness Score			−0.0225	0.881				
Median House Value					0.0074	0.256	0.0055	0.431
Cultural Amenities			2.000E-04	0.104			0.0003	0.012**
Recreational Amenities			1.8000E-05	0.947			−0.0002	0.517
Climate			2.5000E-03	0.133			−2.2359	0.015**
R-square	0.6502		0.7281		0.6720		0.6958	
Adjusted R-square	0.6354		0.6828		0.6497		0.6596	
# of Observation	50		43		48		48	

Note
* significant at 0.10
** significant at 0.05
*** significant at 0.01

effect on talent. In addition, diversity has a direct effect on high-technology industry. When combined, the total effect of diversity on high-technology industry is highly significant. Third, the path analysis suggests that the effects of other variables, such as coolness or other amenity measures, are weak and frequently negative (not shown in Figure 4.5).[40]

Talent and Regional Income

A large and influential body of research notes the close relationship be-tween human capital and income. This work has focused on the direct effects of human capital on income at the regional level.[41] The research presented here builds upon this line of work by examining the effects of human capital or talent on income while controlling for the effects of high-technology industry, diversity, and other factors. The analysis em-ploys two income measures: (1) per capita income and (2) absolute change in per capita income from 1991 to 1997.

Per Capita Income Level

There exists a substantial variation in per capita income among the top 50 MSAs. The top-ranked MSAs are San Francisco and New York, with per capita income levels exceeding U.S.$30,000. But 36 of the top

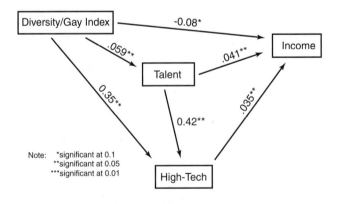

Figure 4.5 Results of path analysis

50 MSAs have per capita incomes below $25,000, and eight of these have per capita income levels below $20,000.

Talent is positively correlated with per capita income, a finding that is in line with the literature (see Table 4.2).[42] The strong positive correlations suggest that places that are open and supportive of diversity will not only attract talent, but tend to have higher income levels as well. Based on this, one can theorize that low entry barriers to talent (represented by the Gay Index) translate into higher regional incomes. Income is also positively correlated with cultural amenities, coolness, and median house values, as well as high-technology industry.

Multivariate regression models were used to further investigate the nature of the relationships between income, talent, and other factors (see Table 4.5), and again the relationship is reasonably positive and robust.[43] The talent coefficient is positively and significantly associated with per capita income level in all permutations of the model. The coefficient for cultural amenities is also positively and significantly associated with per capita income. Per capita income level is also associated with high-technology industry. This suggests that talent and technology work together in creating regional income effects. While this analysis does not address the chicken-or-the-egg question of what comes first—talent or high-technology jobs—it does suggest that talent is an important factor in its own right.

Income Change

It is also useful to examine the relationship between talent and income change between 1991 and 1997. The results of the regression analysis suggest that the relationship is robust (see Table 4.5).[44] Path analysis was used to further probe the structure of relationships among these variables (see Figure 4.5).[45] Taken in combination with the results of the field research, the statistical findings suggest the following set of relationships among these variables: Talent is associated with diversity, as diverse and open environments attract high-human capital individuals. Diversity is directly associated with talent and also with concentrations of high-technology industry. High-technology industry is attracted to places with high levels of human capital and high levels of diversity.

Table 4.5 Regression Model Findings: Talent and Income Change

Dependent Variable: Per-Capita Income — Per-Capita Income Change

VARIABLES	Model 1		Model 2		Model 3	
	COEFFICIENT	P-VALUE	COEFFICIENT	P-VALUE	COEFFICIENT	P-VALUE
Diversity	−640.33	0.244			−201.5561	0.3780
High-Tech	911.88	0.001***	549.60	0.048**	177.3669	0.1100
Talent	27629.77	0.005***	24958.17	0.028**	8782.428	0.0310**
Coolness Score (POV)			−236.73	0.348		
Median House Value	−9.59	0.399	−22.36	0.101	−14.3988	0.0040***
Cultural Amenities			0.91	0.001***		
Recreational Amenities			0.93	0.758		
Climate			−22.36	0.101		
R-square	0.6028		0.7114		0.2909	
Adjusted R-square	0.5659		0.6520		0.225	
# of Observation	48		42		48	

Note
* significant at 0.10
** significant at 0.05
*** significant at 0.01

Talent and high-technology industry work independently and in concert to generate higher regional incomes. Talent is thus a key intermediate variable in attracting high-technology industries and generating higher regional incomes.

Summary

These findings have a number of implications for regional development. Taken together with the work of Jacobs and Lucas and the empirical findings of Glaeser and others, they suggest that talent, or human capital, is perhaps the driving factor in regional development. Going beyond this literature, however, they further suggest that talent is not just an endowment or stock that is in place in a given region, but that certain regional conditions are required to attract talent. In other words, talent does not simply show up in a region; rather, certain regional factors appear to play a role in creating an environment or habitat that can produce, attract, and retain talent or human capital.

Paramount among these factors, the findings suggest, is openness to diversity or low barriers to entry for talent. This, in turn, suggests that a more efficacious approach to regional development may be to emphasize policies and programs to attract human capital, as opposed to conventional approaches that focus on the attraction of firms and the formation of industrial clusters. Regions may have much to gain by investing in a people climate as a complement to their more traditional business climate strategies. It also appears that diversity has a significant impact on a region's ability to attract talent and to generate high-technology industries. Thus, regions would appear to have much to gain by introducing measures to support and enhance diversity. This suggests that diversity is more than just a social goal—it may have direct economic benefits as well.

PART II
TOLERANCE

5
BOHEMIA AND ECONOMIC GEOGRAPHY

"What are the external facts in regard to the life in Bohemia, the half-world, the red-light district and other 'moral regions' less pronounced in character?"
—*Robert Park*

"Hip is how business understands itself."
—*Tom Frank*

"When the going gets weird, the weird turn pro."
—*Hunter S. Thompson*

Introduction

In spring of 2000, *The Economist* ran an article titled, "The Geography of Cool." It highlighted the connection between bohemian enclaves in places like New York City, London, and Berlin—and their abilities to attract people, harness their creativity energy, spawn new innovations and generate economic growth. Economists and geographers have noted the role of cites as centers of innovation, while sociologists and cultural theorists have explored bohemian lifestyles and culture, but little if any serious research has addressed the connection between cultural assets, human capital, and innovative industries. It is precisely that connection that is the subject of this chapter.

Scholars have long noted the role played by bohemia in modern societies. Robert Park identified the importance of bohemia and what can be referred to as *subcultural capital* to both society in general and cities in particular.[1] Caesar Grana noted the historical distinction between bohemia and bourgeois.[2] David Brooks suggested that the traditional distinction between the bourgeois and bohemia has given way to a new blending he calls the bohemian-bourgeois—*bobos* for short.[3]

Jacobs long ago identified the connection between creativity, bohemian diversity, and vibrant city life.[4] More recently, geographers and other social scientists have focused on the role of culture and subculture in consumption patterns. Geographers have done a great deal of work on the role of gentrification in artistic communities in shaping city development.[5] Still others have probed the role of lifestyle and cultural amenities in city life, the attraction of human capital, and economic growth.[6] A recent study examined the creative economy in New England, and found evidence of a relationship between creative activity associated with bohemians and creative economic outcomes more generally.[7]

Despite these important contributions, the literature has neglected the geography of bohemia and its relationship to other regional characteristics and outcomes. Some of this neglect can be attributed to a lack of reliable measures of bohemia, as well as a conceptual framework which links bohemia to other factors associated with innovation and economic growth.

In fact, we can now measure the relationships between bohemia, human capital, and high-technology industry. The Bohemian Index directly measures the bohemian population at the MSA level. Statistical research deriving from this measure reveals the relationships between geographic concentrations of bohemians, talent, and high-technology industry concentration. The results show that the presence and concentration of bohemians in an area creates an environment or milieu that attracts other types of talented or high human-capital individuals. The presence of such human capital concentrations in a region in turn attracts and generates innovative technology-based industries.

The results also indicate that the geography of bohemia is highly concentrated. While diversity maintains the strongest connection to high-tech industry and talent, the relationship between the Bohemian Index and concentrations of high-human-capital individuals and such industry is also very strong.

Concepts and Theories

The literature on bohemia is vast. For our purposes, two strands of this literature are particularly useful. The first considers the economic, social, and cultural distinctions between bohemians and mainstream or bourgeois society. Once a hard and fast distinction, recent writing points to a possible blending of these two categories. The second considers cities as centers of creative human activity and points toward a connection between cultural amenities, creativity, and economic growth.

Bohemian and Bourgeois

Decades ago, Caesar Grana drew a distinction between bohemian and bourgeoisie,[8] noting that bohemians exist in a world outside the traditional Protestant ethic of capitalism, prefer more libertine lifestyles, and favor enjoyment and self-actualization over work. Sociologist Daniel Bell placed the tradeoff of enjoyment and work as the center of his thesis on the cultural contradictions of capitalism.[9] In his words, "not work but lifestyle became the source of satisfaction and criterion for desirable behavior in the society. What has happened in society in the last 50 years —as a result of the erosion of the religious ethic and the increase in discretionary income—*is that culture has taken the initiative in promoting change*, and the economy has been geared to meeting those wants [his emphasis]."[10]

More recent writing draws from these ideal types to suggest their possible synthesis. Jon Seabrook points to the rise of so-called *no-brow* culture, which overcomes the old distinction between high and low culture.[11] Brooks suggests the rise of a new category that he dubs the bohemian-bourgeois, or "bobos," as a new social grouping. While Brooks recognizes the rise of this new kind of lifestyle, he neglects the underlying economic shifts that made it possible.[12] Simply put, he fails to see this new grouping in connection to underlying economic trends, particularly the rise of the knowledge economy. The increasing importance of creativity, innovation, and knowledge in the economy opens up the social space where more eccentric, alternative, or bohemian types of people can be integrated into core economic and social institutions. Capitalism—or, more accurately, new forms of capitalist enterprise (i.e., the R&D lab and the startup company)—are extending their reach in ways that integrate formerly marginalized individuals and social groups into the value creation process.

Others are critical of this process. The historian and social critic Tom Frank suggests that this synthesis is linked to the evolution of capitalism, and refers to the conquest of cool—the blending of business culture and counterculture into a new culture of hip consumerism.[13] "Consumer capitalism did not demand conformity or homogeneity," writes Frank, "rather, it thrived on the doctrine of liberation and continual transgression that is still familiar today." Far from being an oppositional movement, capitalism has absorbed and integrated what used to be thought of as alternative or cool.

Taken as a whole, this literature is suggestive of a growing connection between bohemia and mainstream society, and of a growing integration of bohemian symbols and culture into mainstream economic activity. This lends support to our thesis of the relationship between concentrations of bohemians and the clustering of other creative forms of economic activity.

Bohemia and Geography

Urban sociologists have examined the role of bohemia in the social structure of cities and called attention to the role of cultural and subcultural capital in modern society. Park long ago noted the role of subcultures such as bohemia in the social and spatial structure of cities.[14] For Park, vibrant cities developed outlets for eccentric lifestyles and alternative cultures—places where subcultural groups find identity and constitute the broad schema of city life. Many others have built upon Park's theories, suggesting that bohemian subcultures play an important role in both societies in general and cities in particular. This line of theory and research identifies subculture as an important and stabilizing element of society.

Urbanists have noted the importance of diversity and creativity as a key factor in city growth and development. In her classic work on cities, Jacobs called attention to the role of creativity and diversity as *engines* for city growth.[15] She noted the significance of eclecticism and inventiveness as important components of city life. She also highlighted the role of older, underutilized buildings of the sort associated with bohemian enclaves as important spaces of innovation, writing that, "New Ideas occur in old buildings."

Economic geographers and regional scientists have examined the role of cultural amenities in firm location and regional growth. There exists now a considerable literature on the role of cities as entertainment and lifestyle centers. Hannigan has noted the rise of the Fantasy City—which uses entertainment and lifestyle to attract people.[16] Terry Clark and Richard Lloyd argue that amenities are a key component of modern cities, referring to this lifestyle-oriented city as an Entertainment Machine.[17] Joel Kotkin identified the relationships between lifestyle amenities and the locational preferences of some high-technology industries for neighborhoods such as New York's Silicon Alley, San Francisco's SOMA and Mission Districts, and Seattle's Pioneer Square.[18] One report found that some fifty percent of high-technology firms and employment in the Seattle region is located in a high-amenity district surrounding the city's urban core. In an ironic twist, a growing concern exists that high-technology firms and industries are displacing bohemian enclaves in cities like New York and San Francisco.

This body of work suggests a connection between bohemian centers and creative activity in general, and calls attention to the tendency for innovative economic activity to increasingly cluster in and around bohemian enclaves.

Research Design

Building on these insights, this research was derived from an empirical analysis of the geography of bohemia and the relationship of concentrations of bohemians to concentrations of human capital and to clusters of high-technology industries. Qualitative research—through interviews and focus groups—allowed for a better understanding of the structure and mechanics of these relationships, and made it possible to generate testable hypotheses.[19] The interview and focus group research buttressed the quantitative research, indicating that cultural and lifestyle factors are an important component of these location decisions, suggesting in particular the importance of bohemian communities to those decisions.

The accompanying statistical analysis examined both the geography and the relationship of that observed geography to other characteristics of regional economies. Descriptive statistics, correlation or bivariate analysis, and multivariate regression analysis all provided the necessary information for the Bohemian Index (described below).

The Bohemian Index is based on occupational data from the *1990 U.S. Decennial Census Public Use Microdata Sample* (1% and 5%). It includes the following occupations: authors (183), designers (182), musicians and composers (186), actors and directors (187), craft-artists, painters, sculptors, and artist printmakers (188), photographers (189), dancers (193), and artists, performers, and related workers (194). The Index is basically a location quotient that measures the percentage of bohemians in a region compared to the national population of bohemians divided by the percent of total population in a region compared to the total national population.

This index is an improvement over previous measures of cultural and lifestyle amenities in that it represents a direct measure of the *producers* of cultural and creative assets. It also avoids the pitfalls of other, more indirect measures, which tend merely to tally up cultural assets (i.e., measures of cultural programming, art museums and galleries, or restaurants) and which draw distinctions between so-called high and low culture. Table 5.1 provides descriptive statistics for the Bohemian Index and other key measures used in this analysis.

Table 5.1 Descriptive Statistics for Key Variables

	Obs	Mean	Std Dev	Min	Max
Boho Index	50	1.15	0.28	0.70	1.93
Techpole	50	1.40	1.88	0.06	8.24
Talent Index	50	0.24	0.05	0.14	0.42
Coolness	43	6.35	1.51	1.00	10.00
Culture	50	1,804.76	1,458.98	482.00	9,375.56
Gay Index	50	1.32	0.87	0.19	5.39
Melting Pot	50	0.08	0.07	0.01	0.39
Population	50	2,356,307.00	2,888,147.00	716,419.00	16,000,000.00

To examine the robustness of the Bohemian Index, we compared it to other measures of amenities. The first group includes traditional measures of indicators of artistic and cultural amenities, adapted from the *Places Rated Almanac*.[20] The culture measure is a composite based on the following factors: radio broadcast time devoted to classical music, public television stations, public library book acquisitions, nonprofit art museums and galleries, performances of fine arts and musical groups, and access to the culture of adjacent urban areas. The correlation between the Bohemian Index and this measure is robust.[21] (see Table 5.2). A less traditional amenity measure is the so-called coolness factor, developed by a *POV Magazine*, which measures the percentage of population ages 22 to 29, the diversity of this cohort, nightlife, and culture. The correlation between it and the Bohemian Index is also high.[22]

Human Capital: The *Talent Index* is a measure of highly educated people, defined as those with a bachelor's degree and above. It is normalized on a percentage basis or per thousand people, and based on the *1990 U.S. Decennial Census Public Use Microdata Sample.*

Diversity/Openness: To examine the relationship between bohemians and other dimensions of openness and diversity, the research employs several alternative measures of diversity. The first is a *Melting Pot Index* based on the percentage of population that is foreign born. It is normalized per thousand people and based on the *1990 U.S. Decennial Census Public Use Microdata Sample.*

Table 5.2 Correlation Matrix

	BOHO	TECHPOLE	TALENT	COOLNESS	CULTURE	GAY	MELTING POT	POP
Boho Index	1							
TechPole	0.654	1						
Talent	0.553	0.723	1					
Coolness	0.512	0.423	0.467	1				
Culture	0.541	0.493	0.423	0.569	1			
Gay Index	0.600	0.768	0.718	0.377	0.289	1		
Melting Pot	0.505	0.427	0.206	0.320	0.422	0.492	1	
Population	0.602	0.485	0.233	0.414	0.850	0.293	0.599	1

The second is the *Gay Index*, also based on data from the *1990 U.S. Decennial Census Public Use Microdata Sample*, and identifying households in which a householder and an unmarried partner were both of the same sex (in this case, male). Approximately 0.01 percent of the population was composed of gay coupled men. The index is basically a location quotient that measures the percentage of gay households compared to the national population of gay households divided by the percent of total population in a city compared to the total national population.

An important component of the analysis examines the effect of bohemians on high-technology industry (controlling for other factors). The measure of high-tech industry concentration is based on the Milken Institute's *Tech-Pole Index*, a composite measure derived from the percent of national high-tech real output multiplied by the high-tech real output location quotient for each MSA.

Following from this, we used both bivariate and multivariate analyses to examine the effect of bohemians (again, controlling for other factors) on human capital, and high-technology industry location. The analysis is based on the 50 largest metropolitan regions (MSAs)—those with populations of 700,000 and above. For most regions, the metropolitan statistical area or MSA is employed as the unit of analysis. The consolidated metropolitan statistical area or CMSA is used as the unit of analysis for the five largest regions: San Francisco, Los Angeles, Miami-Fort Lauderdale, New York, and Dallas-Fort Worth, to account for broad commuting patterns in those regions.

The Geography of Bohemia

Let's begin with a basic picture of the economic geography of bohemia. To do so, Figure 5.1 provides a map of the geographic distribution of bohemians in the United States. As these data show, the geography of bohemia is highly concentrated and uneven. [Appendix A provides a listing of all 50 MSAs ranked by the total number of bohemians and bohemians per capita as well as the Bohemian Index].

Not surprisingly, New York City and Los Angeles top the list in terms of total number of bohemians. Both have bohemian populations

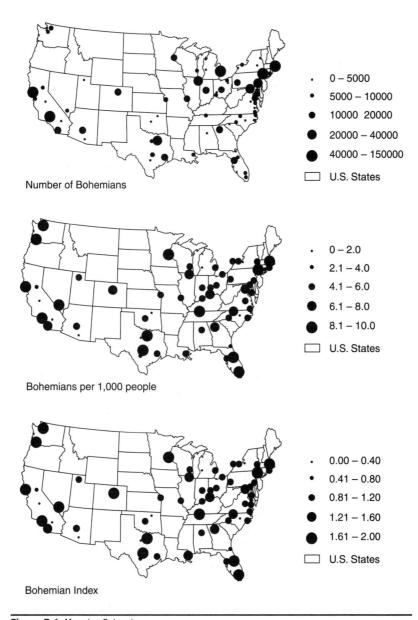

Figure 5.1 Mapping Bohemia

in excess of 100,000. San Francisco is next with a population of more than 40,000 bohemians (roughly a third the size of the two largest regions). Chicago and Washington, D.C., have bohemian populations in excess of

30,000, and another 12 or so regions have bohemian populations that exceed 10,000 people. Some 28 regions have bohemian populations less than 5,000. The differences between the highest- and lowest-ranked regions are quite considerable. The highest-ranked regions have bohemian populations that are some 25 times larger than those of the lowest-ranked. Obviously, this simple count measure is likely to be affected by the population size of the MSA. (In fact, the correlation between the Bohemian Index and population size is 0.60.) (See Table 5.2.)

A simple way to control for this is to normalize by population size. When this is done, Seattle, New York, and Los Angeles top the list with more than 9 bohemians per thousand people. Six regions have more than 8 bohemians per thousand: Nashville, Portland, Oregon, Washington, D.C., Minneapolis-St. Paul, San Francisco, Boston, and Austin. Five regions have more than 7 bohemians per thousand; and an additional eight have more than six bohemians per thousand. Nearly half of the sample MSAs have between four and six bohemians per thousand people. The lowest-ranked regions include: San Antonio, Oklahoma City, Buffalo, Cleveland, Pittsburgh, Albany, and Baltimore.

The Bohemian Index is a location quotient measure, essentially a ratio that compares the percentage of bohemians in a region to the national pattern. An index value of 1.0 means these shares are in exact proportion. An index value of greater than one means a greater than average concentration, while a value of less than one means a less than average concentration. The average for the top 50 MSAs on the Bohemian Index is 1.15.

The two leading regions on the Bohemian Index are New York and Los Angeles, whose Bohemian Index values exceed 1.85. Five regions have Bohemian Index values in excess of 1.5: Washington, D.C., San Francisco, Seattle, Boston, and Nashville. Another three regions—Austin; Portland, Oregon; and Minneapolis—have Bohemian Index values in excess of 1.4. Eight additional regions have Bohemian Index values above the MSA average of 1.15. However, 31 MSAs have Bohemian Index values less than the MSA average, and 17 of these have Bohemian Index values of less than one. The six lowest-ranked regions—Cleveland, Albany, Pittsburgh, San Antonio, Oklahoma City, and Buffalo—have Bohemian Index values in the 0.7 to 0.8 range, less than half that of the leading regions.

Talent/Human Capital

With this basic descriptive exercise in mind, I turn attention to the relationship between bohemia and talent or human capital. Recall the main hypothesis is that the presence of a large concentration of bohemians signals a regional milieu that is attractive to and supportive of other types of human capital. To get at this, I look first at the direct relationship between bohemia and human capital, and then turn to other measures of openness and diversity.

The findings suggest a rather strong relationship between bohemia and human capital. First off, seven of the top 10 Bohemian Index regions also number among the top 10 MSAs in terms of human capital: Washington, D.C., San Francisco, New York City, Seattle, Boston, Austin, and Minneapolis. On the opposite side of the spectrum, seven of the lowest-ranked Bohemian Index regions also rank among the lowest on the Talent Index: Louisville, Tampa, Dayton, Cleveland, Pittsburgh, San Antonio, and Buffalo.[23] Figure 5.2 is a scatter plot that shows the relationship between the Bohemian Index and the Talent Index for sample MSAs. Washington, D.C., Boston, San Francisco, Seattle, Austin, Atlanta, and New York occupy the upper right-hand quadrant of this graph.

Figure 5.3 is a graph that plots the correlation coefficients between human capital and the Bohemian Index. As this figure shows, a striking relationship exists between the Bohemian Index and human capital (measured as various levels of education attainment). The correlation coefficients between these two measures rise sharply alongside level of education. Furthermore, the correlation coefficients are highly positive for highly educated individuals (measured as the percentage of the population with a bachelor's or graduate degree) and negative for other segments of population (measured as the percentage of the population with a high school degree or less).

The presence of a large concentration of bohemians may indicate an underlying openness to diversity. In fact, a main hypothesis of this research is that the presence of a significant bohemia population is a signal of such openness. This buttresses what the preceding chapter shows: that a key factor in regional development is *low entry barriers* that this sort of openness to diversity indicates.

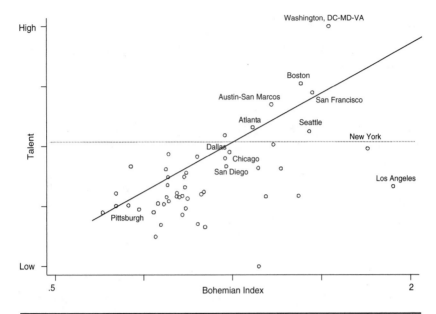

Figure 5.2 Bohemian Index and talent

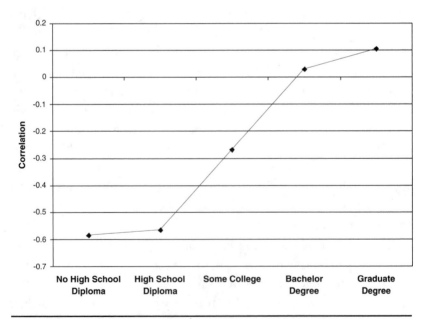

Figure 5.3 Correlations between Bohemian Index and level of education

To explain this connection, I examined the relationship between the Bohemian Index and two measures of diversity: the Gay Index and the Melting Pot index. The results suggest a close association among these factors. Six of the top 10 Bohemian Index cities also number among the top 10 Gay Index cities: San Francisco, Washington, D.C., Austin, Seattle, Los Angeles, and Boston. Five of the top 10 Bohemian Index regions also number among the top 10 Melting Pot Index regions: Los Angeles, New York, San Francisco, Boston, and Washington, D.C.[24]

To get a better grasp of the relationship between bohemians and human capital, multivariate regressions were conducted with talent as a dependent variable and the Bohemian Index as one of a series of independent variables. The regressions examined the relationships between talent and the Bohemian Index, controlling for other amenity measures (i.e., culture, recreation, climate), openness factors (i.e., Gay Index, Melting Pot Index), population size, and median house value. The results of these regression models are presented in Table 5.3. Generally speaking, the findings here are robust and suggest a close relationship between the Bohemian Index and talent.[25]

The main findings are clear. A close association exists between bohemia and talent. The presence of a significant concentration of bohemians indicates an environment that is open and attractive to high human capital individuals.

High Technology

With these findings in mind, I now turn attention to the relationship between bohemia and a particular form of innovative and creative activity—that associated with high-technology industry. For this purpose, I looked at the direct association between bohemian clusters and concentrations of high-technology industry.

The findings here suggest a close association between bohemian clusters and high-technology industry. Six of the top 10 bohemian regions also number among the top 10 high-tech regions (based on the Milken Tech-pole Index): San Francisco, Boston, Seattle, Washington, D.C., Los Angeles, and New York. The correlation between the Bohemian Index and the Tech-pole Index is quite high (see Table 5.2).[26]

Table 5.3 Regression Results: Bohemian Index and Talent

VARIABLES	Model 1			Model 2	
	COEFFICIENT	P-VALUE		COEFFICIENT	P-VALUE
Boho Index	0.058	0.012**		0.057	0.007***
Gay Index	0.031	0.000***		0.031	0.000***
Population	0.000	0.000***		0.000	0.000***
Cultural amenities	0.000	0.000***		0.000	0.000***
Recreation	0.000	0.000***		0.000	0.002***
Climate	0.000	0.795		0.000	0.682
Coolness Index	0.001			0.805	
R-square	0.789			0.764	
Adjusted R-square	0.747			0.731	
# of Observations	43			50	

Note: * Significant at 0.10 level
** Significant at 0.05 level
*** Significant at 0.01 level

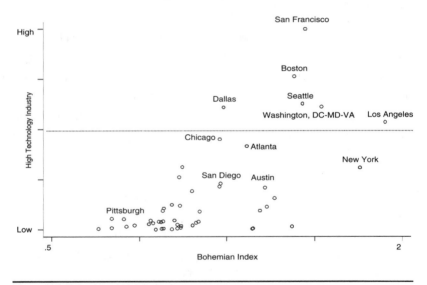

Figure 5.4 Bohemia and high technology

Figure 5.4 is a scatter plot that shows the relationship between the Bohemian Index and the Tech-pole Index for sample MSAs. San Francisco, Boston, Seattle, Washington, D.C., and Los Angeles occupy the upper right-hand quadrant of this graph.

Table 5.4 Regression Results: Bohemian Index and High Technology

VARIABLES	Model 1		Model 2		Model 3		Model 4	
	COEFFICIENT	P-VALUE	COEFFICIENT	P-VALUE	COEFFICIENT	P-VALUE	COEFFICIENT	P-VALUE
Boho Index	2.055	0.008***	2.492	0.001***	2.133	0.024**	1.695	0.030**
Gay Index	1.265	0.000***					0.866	0.003***
Talent			20.315	0.000***	21.367	0.000***	10.611	0.038**
Median House Value					0.003	0.667	0.003	0.625
Coolness Index					−0.021	0.891		
R-square	0.6478		0.6161		0.6488		0.7064	
Adjusted R-square	0.6329		0.5998		0.6108		0.6791	
# of Observations	50		50		42		48	

Note: * Significant at 0.10 level
** Significant at 0.05 level
*** Significant at 0.01 level

To better explain the relationship between bohemian clusters and high-technology industry, we conducted multivariate regressions with the Tech-pole Index as the dependent variable and the Bohemian Index as one of a series of independent variables. The regressions examined the relationships between high-technology industry concentrations and the Bohemian Index, controlling for talent, other amenity measures (i.e. culture, recreation, climate), openness factors (i.e., Gay Index, Melting Pot Index), population size, and median house value. The results of these regression models are presented in Table 5.4.

Summary

Generally speaking, the findings here are robust and suggest a close relationship between the Bohemian Index and talent. The Bohemian Index is a strong and unambiguous predictor of high-technology industry concentrations. The results of the various models suggest a robust and positive relationship.[27]

Bohemia, then, means more for the larger economy—particularly the most advanced economic sectors—than is generally perceived. The geography of bohemia is highly concentrated. And there are significant and positive relationships between the Bohemian Index and both high-human-capital individuals and concentrations of high-technology industry, with the latter relationship particularly strong.

In sum, the mechanisms underlying these findings work more or less in the following way: The presence of a significant bohemian concentration in a region indicates an environment that is open and attractive to high human capital individuals. This in turn stimulates the kind of creativity and innovation associated with high-technology industries. The urban regions that have resulted are the most economically dynamic urban regions in the contemporary United States. Like the *avant-garde* traditionally associated with bohemia, such cities are the advance guard of the new place-based creative economy.

6

TECHNOLOGY AND TOLERANCE

(with Gary Gates)

In previous chapters, I discussed individual attributes that successful cities and regions possess—quality of place, large bohemian populations, and receptivity to immigrants and other diverse populations. This chapter looks in even greater detail at the role of diversity or tolerance in high-technology industry concentration and growth. We have already seen that regions possessing an abundance of talent—human capital—grow stronger and faster than those lacking talent. But just as important to that growth is another factor: the forces that attract talented knowledge workers who, because of their skills, can pick from a wide range of places when deciding where to locate. Chief among the attractions to these workers is diversity and a generalized acceptance of diversity among the local population.

As mentioned earlier, the driving forces in the growth and development of cities and regions can be found in the productivity gains associated with the clustering of talented people or human capital.[1] And there is ample empirical evidence of the close association between human capital and regional economic growth.[2] Indeed, the statistical correlations between the percentage of the population with at least a college education and the strength of the high-tech economy are uniformly high and significant.[3] (See Appendix A for a more detailed discussion). Hence, the statement by McKinsey and Company (the management-consulting firm) that the war for talent is the number one competitive issue facing companies in the United States and around the world is hardly surprising. It remains the pre-eminent concern even though the Internet bubble has burst.[4]

What, then, brings talented workers to a particular metropolitan area? How do they make their residential decisions? What role do diversity and tolerance play?

Our theory is that a connection exists between a metropolitan area's level of tolerance for a range of people, its ethnic and social diversity, and its success in attracting talented people, including high-technology workers. People in technology businesses are drawn to places known for diversity of thought and open-mindedness—places with low barriers to entry for human capital.

We examined the potential relationship between our measures of diversity and tolerance and high-technology success in the 50 most populated metropolitan areas in the United States.[5] To do this, we utilized three indices to attempt to capture the level of diversity and tolerance within the nation's most populous metropolitan areas. All the indices utilize the *1990 U.S. Decennial Census Public Use Microdata Sample.*[6] We built from the three basic diversity indices—the Gay Index,[7] the Bohemian Index, and the Foreign-born Index—a Composite Diversity Index, which is a sum of the three individual measures.

We then compared our diversity measures to the Milken Institute's 1998 Tech-Pole measure, whose metro region rankings derived from two factors: (1) the output of an area's high-tech industries expressed as a percentage of the output of the nation's high-tech industries, and (2) a ratio of the amount of a metropolitan area's output from high-tech industries to the amount of the nation's output from high-tech industries.[8]

The first measure favors large metropolitan areas; the second favors small areas with large technology sectors. By multiplying them, the Milken Index creates a measure that favors neither. The term "tech-pole" refers to the relative gravitational pull that a metropolitan area exerts on high-tech industries. This measure is used throughout the study to compare a metropolitan area's technology prowess with our measures of talent, tolerance, and diversity.

We also compared our measures with the Milken Institute's Tech-Growth Index.[9] This measures growth in output of high-tech industries within metropolitan areas from 1990 to 1998 relative to the national growth rate in output of high-tech industries during the same period. (All 50 metropolitan areas, ranked by our indices and the Milken measures, are shown in the Appendix along with statistical techniques and modeling.[10])

Somewhat surprisingly, the leading indicator of a metropolitan area's high-technology success was a large gay population. Gays, as we like to say, can be thought of as *canaries* of the creative economy, and serve as a strong signal of a diverse, progressive environment. Indeed, gays are frequently cited as harbingers of redevelopment and gentrification in distressed urban neighborhoods. The presence of gays in a metropolitan area also provides a barometer for a broad spectrum of amenities attractive to adults, especially those without children.[11]

Utilizing 1990 Census data, we used the Gay Index, which measures the concentration of gays in a community relative to the population in general.[12] Eleven of the top 15 high-tech metropolitan areas also appear in the top 15 of the Gay Index (see Table 6.1). The five metropolitan areas with the highest concentration of gay residents are all among the nation's top 15 high-technology areas: San Francisco, Washington, D.C., Austin, Atlanta, and San Diego.

In all of our statistical analyses, the Gay Index does better than other individual measures of social and cultural diversity as a predictor of high-tech location and high-tech growth (see Appendix). The correlations are exceedingly high and consistently positive and significant.[13] The results of a variety of multivariate regression analyses back this up.[14]

Gays not only predict the concentration of high-tech industry, they are also a predictor of its growth. Five of the cities that rank in the top ten for high-technology growth from 1990 to 1998 rank in the top 10 of the Gay Index. In addition, the correlation between the Gay Index (measured in 1990) and the Milken Tech-Pole Index calculated for 1990 to 2000 increases over time, as shown in Figure 6.1. Figure 6.1 also suggests that the benefits of diversity may actually compound over time by increasing a region's high-tech prosperity.

Table 6.1 Milken Tech-Pole Ranking and Gay Index. Top and Bottom 15 Out of Fifty Metropolitan Areas.

MILKEN TECH-POLE RANKING	METROPOLITAN AREA	GAY INDEX RANKING
	TOP 15 RANKINGS	
1	San Francisco	1
2	Boston	8
3	Seattle	6
4	Washington	2
5	Dallas	19
6	Los Angeles	7
7	Chicago	15
8	Atlanta	4
9	Phoenix	22
10	New York	14
11	Philadelphia	36
12	San Diego	5
13	Denver	10
14	Austin	3
15	Houston	21
	BOTTOM 15 RANKINGS	
36	Cleveland	47
37	Miami	12
38	Rochester	13
39	Albany	30
40	Nashville	28
41	Greensboro	46
42	Oklahoma City	27
43	Las Vegas	48
44	Norfolk	37
45	Richmond	29
46	Buffalo	50
47	New Orleans	24
48	Honolulu	20
49	Memphis	33
50	Louisville	42

Source: Milken Institute Tech-Pole Ratings; Gay Index constructed by Richard Florida and Gary Gates using data from 1990 U.S. Decennial Census Public Use Microdata Sample (5%)

We also examine how the concentration of gays in combination with other factors affects high-tech growth. A metropolitan area's percentage of gay residents provides the only significant predictor of high-tech growth in a region when we factor in other regional characteristics such

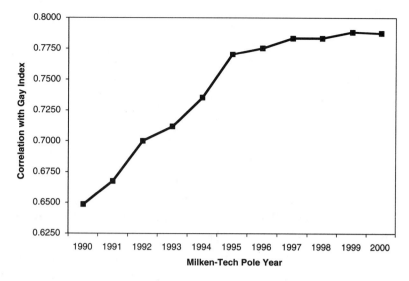

Source: Milken Institute "Tech-Pole" Ratings; Gay Index constructed by Richard Florida and Gary J. Gates using data from 1990 U.S. Decennial Census Public Use Microdata Sample (5%)

Figure 6.1 Correlation between Gay Index and the high-tech industry, 1990–2000

as talent, foreign born, bohemians, several measures of lifestyle amenities, and population.[15]

Statistically, one might be concerned that the influence of San Francisco (which ranks unusually high on both the high-tech and gay indices) may create a false association between the two measures. To check for this, we removed San Francisco from the data and repeated the analyses. The basic findings remain virtually the same.[16] In fact, the influence of the Gay Index on high-tech growth strengthens slightly when San Francisco is not included. This increases our confidence in the strength of the concentration of gays as a predictor of high-technology concentration and growth.

While our findings on the link between the Gay Index and high-tech growth cannot be viewed as conclusive, the results are consistent with our theory that social and cultural diversity attracts talent and stimulates high-tech growth.[17] These findings support the view that encouraging diversity and low barriers to entry can help to attract human capital and generate technology-based growth.

Like gays, high concentrations of culturally creative people—bohemians—are also an indicator of a metropolitan area's high-technology performance (as discussed in Chapter 3). The Bohemian Index, which measures the number of writers, designers, musicians, actors and directors, painters and sculptors, photographers, and dancers found in a metropolitan area, is a considerable improvement over traditional measures of amenities (such as restaurants, museums, symphonies and the like) in that it provides a direct measure of the producers of those amenities.[18] Metropolitan areas that are over-represented by these bohemians are those with an appreciation and acceptance for amenities that support and showcase creativity and artistic expression.

As the previous chapters showed, there is a strong correlation be-tween the Bohemian Index and the concentration and strength of high-tech industry.[19] Ten of the top 15 bohemian metropolitan areas also number among the nation's top 15 high-technology areas, notably Seattle, Los Angeles, New York, Washington, San Francisco, and Boston (see Table 6.2).[20] Thirteen out of the bottom 15 high-tech met-ropolitan areas fail to appear in the top 15 of the Boho Index.

Finally, metropolitan areas with high concentrations of foreign-born residents rank high as technology centers. The Milken Institute's list of *Melting Pot Metros* ranks the most ethnically diverse regions in the country. Sure enough, highly ranked regions in California and Texas, as well as Chicago, Washington, D.C., and New York City are also hot spots of economic growth.[21] Not surprisingly, these metropolitan areas are also ranked highly as regions of technology and technological growth.[22]

Leading high-tech centers are places where people from virtually any background can settle and thrive. In Silicon Valley, the world's leading high-tech center, nearly a quarter of the population is foreign born; and almost one-third of the Valley's high-tech scientists and engineers hail from foreign countries, according to research by Annalee Saxenian.[23] Roughly one-quarter of new Silicon Valley businesses established since 1980 had a Chinese or Indian-born founder. That figure increased to more than 30 percent between 1995 and 1999. And, these figures may actually underestimate the extent of immigrant influence, because firms started with a non-Asian co-founder are not counted in Saxenian's study.

To look more closely at the role of ethnic diversity in high-technology concentration, we examine the relationship between high-tech industry and the percent of a region's population that is foreign born. Nine of the

Table 6.2 Milken Tech-Pole Ranking and Boho Index. Top and Bottom 15 Out of 50 Metropolitan Areas.

MILKEN TECH-POLE RANK	METROPOLITAN AREA	BOHO INDEX RANK
	TOP 15 REGIONS	
1	San Francisco	8
2	Boston	9
3	Seattle	1
4	Washington	6
5	Dallas	15
6	Los Angeles	2
7	Chicago	20
8	Atlanta	13
9	Phoenix	24
10	New York	3
11	Philadelphia	35
12	San Diego	18
13	Denver	14
14	Austin	10
15	Houston	30
	BOTTOM 15 RANKINGS	
36	Cleveland	47
37	Miami	27
38	Rochester	31
39	Albany	45
40	Nashville	4
41	Greensboro	21
42	Oklahoma City	49
43	Las Vegas	11
44	Norfolk	37
45	Richmond	26
46	Buffalo	48
47	New Orleans	41
48	Honolulu	17
49	Memphis	40
50	Louisville	33

Source: Milken Institute Tech-Pole Ratings; Bohemian Index constructed by Richard Florida and Gary Gates using data from 1990 U.S. Decennial Census Public Use Microdata Sample (5%)

top 15 (and 8 out of the top 10) metropolitan areas, in terms of foreign-born residents, were also among the nation's top 15 high-technology areas: Los Angeles, New York, San Francisco, San Diego, Chicago, Houston, Boston, Washington, and Seattle (see Table 6.3).

Table 6.3 Milken Tech-Pole Ranking and Foreign-Born Index. Top and Bottom 15 Out of Fifty Metropolitan Areas.

MILKEN TECH-POLE RANK	METROPOLITAN AREA	FOREIGN-BORN RANK
TOP 15 REGIONS		
1	San Francisco	4
2	Boston	9
3	Seattle	15
4	Washington	10
5	Dallas	16
6	Los Angeles	2
7	Chicago	7
8	Atlanta	31
9	Phoenix	21
10	New York	3
11	Philadelphia	25
12	San Diego	6
13	Denver	29
14	Austin	19
15	Houston	8
BOTTOM 15 RANKINGS		
36	Cleveland	22
37	Miami	1
38	Rochester	24
39	Albany	30
40	Nashville	47
41	Greensboro	48
42	Oklahoma City	36
43	Las Vegas	13
44	Norfolk	32
45	Richmond	39
46	Buffalo	27
47	New Orleans	26
48	Honolulu	5
49	Memphis	46
50	Louisville	49

Source: Milken Institute Tech-Pole Ratings; Foreign-Born Index constructed by Richard Florida and Gary Gates using data from 1990 U.S. Decennial Census Public Use Microdata Sample (5%)

Twelve of the bottom 15 high-tech areas do not rank in the top 15 on the Foreign-born Index (although Miami ranked number one). The statistical correlation between percentage foreign-born and high-technology success was quite strong.[24]

While the relationship between immigrants and high technology is encouraging, it is often said that diversity in high-tech industry is somewhat narrow, in the sense that it does not include a high percentage of some racial minorities, such as African-Americans. To get at this issue, we explored the relationship between high-tech industry and the percentage of population that is non-white. The results are, frankly, disturbing. We find no significant correlation here whatsoever.[25]

Social, cultural, and ethnic diversity are strong indicators of a metropolitan area's high-technology success. Our argument about diversity, then, is simple and straightforward. Diversity of human capital is a key component of the ability to attract and retain high-technology industry. To demonstrate this, we constructed a *Composite Diversity Index* (or CDI) based on the three diversity indicators that we discussed earlier— the gay and bohemian indices and the percent of foreign-born residents. We ranked our 50 metropolitan areas by each indicator (low to high) and summed the three rankings.

This CDI strongly correlates with the Milken Tech-Pole Ranking. As Table 6.4 demonstrates, the top 11 metro areas on the CDI are also among the top 15 Milken Tech-Pole regions. The statistical correlation between the Milken Tech-Pole rankings and the CDI rankings is higher than the same correlation with rankings by any of our individual diversity measures, or by simpler measures such as the percentage of college graduates in the population.[26]

Even more compelling, the CDI strongly predicts high-tech growth. When we estimate the effect of the CDI on high-tech growth and factor in the percentage of college graduates in the region, population, and measures of culture, recreation, and climate, we find that our diversity measure has a positive and significant effect on high-tech growth from 1990 to 1998 (see Appendix). These results offer strong evidence of the importance of the combined effects of social, cultural, and ethnic diversity to both high-tech location and growth.

Summary

Tolerance and diversity clearly matter to high-technology concentration and growth. Talented people go to places that have thick labor markets, are open and tolerant, and offer a quality of life they desire.

Table 6.4 Milken Tech-Pole Ranking and Composite Diversity Index. Top and Bottom 15 Out of 50 Metropolitan Areas.

MILKEN TECH-POLE RANK	METROPOLITAN AREA	COMPOSITE DIVERSITY RANK
	TOP 15 REGIONS	
1	San Francisco	2
2	Boston	6
3	Seattle	5
4	Washington	3
5	Dallas	15
6	Los Angeles	1
7	Chicago	11
8	Atlanta	14
9	Phoenix	21
10	New York	4
11	Philadelphia	32
12	San Diego	7
13	Denver	17
14	Austin	8
15	Houston	18
	BOTTOM 15 RANKINGS	
36	Cleveland	43
37	Miami	10
38	Rochester	22
39	Albany	36
40	Nashville	25
41	Greensboro	42
42	Oklahoma City	39
43	Las Vegas	24
44	Norfolk	37
45	Richmond	30
46	Buffalo	48
47	New Orleans	27
48	Honolulu	12
49	Memphis	44
50	Louisville	47

Source: Milken Institute Tech-Pole Ratings; Composite Diversity Index constructed by Richard Florida and Gary Gates using data from 1990 U.S. Decennial Census Public Use Microdata Sample (5%)

And the more diverse and culturally rich, the more attractive they are. Places that attract people attract companies and generate new innovations, and this leads to a virtuous circle of economic growth.

We do not mean to imply that these results prove that a large gay population or concentration of bohemians directly causes the development of a technology industry; the theory is that people in technology businesses are drawn to places known for diversity of thought and open-mindedness, and that our measures potentially get at a broader concept of diversity and inclusiveness.

After all, six metropolitan areas ranked in the top 15 on our three individual indices of diversity. Four of these six metro areas were the top-ranked high-tech regions on the Milken Index—San Francisco, Boston, Seattle, and Washington, D.C. The two remaining regions—Los Angeles and New York—also ranked in the top ten on the Milken Index.

The basic message that other cities and regions should heed is that talent powers economic growth, and diversity and openness attract talent. Companies remain important, but no longer call the shots. The location decisions of people are just as important—potentially more important—than those of firms. In fact, companies increasingly will go where talented people are located.

While more research is certainly required to get at the causal linkages between diversity and high-tech industry, we are convinced by our findings that tolerance and low entry barriers to human capital helps to attract talent and that talent is in turn associated with high-technology industry and regional growth. Cities must begin to combine their goal of providing a better business environment with strategies aimed at improving their diversity and tolerance.

PART III
PLACE

7
THE UNIVERSITY, TALENT,
AND QUALITY OF PLACE

During the 1980s and 1990s, the university was posed as an underutilized weapon in the battle for industrial competitiveness and regional economic growth. Even higher education stalwarts such as Harvard University's then-president Derek Bok argued that the university had a civic duty to ally itself closely with industry to improve productivity. At university after university, new research centers were designed to attract corporate funding, and technology transfer offices were started to commercialize academic breakthroughs.

But we may well have gone too far. Academics and university officials are becoming increasingly concerned that greater involvement in university research is causing a shift from fundamental science to more applied work. Industry, meanwhile, is growing upset over universities' ever more aggressive attempts to profit from industry-funded research through intellectual property rights. In addition, state and local governments are becoming disillusioned that universities are not sparking the kind of regional growth seen in the classic success stories of Stanford University and Silicon Valley in California and of MIT and the Route 128 beltway around Boston. As John Armstrong, former IBM vice president for science and technology, recently noted, policy-makers have overstated the degree to which universities can drive national and regional economies.

Universities have been naively viewed as engines of innovation that pump out new ideas that can be easily translated into commercial innovations and regional growth. This has led to overly mechanistic national and regional policies that seek to commercialize those ideas and transfer them to the private sector. Although there is nothing wrong with these policies that encourage joint research, this view misses the larger economic picture: Universities are far more important as the nation's primary source of knowledge creation and talent. Smart people are the most critical resource to any economy, and especially to the rapidly growing creative economy on which the U.S.'s future rests. Misdirected policies that restrict universities' ability to generate knowledge and attract and produce top talent loom as large threats to the nation's economy. Specific measures such as the landmark Bayh–Dole Act of 1980, which enabled universities to claim ownership of the intellectual property rights generated from federally funded research, have helped universities commercialize innovations but in doing so may have exacerbated the skewing of the university's role.

If federal, state, and local policymakers truly want to leverage universities to spawn economic growth, they must adopt a new view. They have to stop encouraging matches between university and industry for their own sake. Instead, they must focus on strengthening the university's ability to attract the smartest people from around the world—the true wellspring of the creative economy. By attracting these people and rapidly and widely disseminating the knowledge they create, universities will have a much greater effect on the nation's economy as well as regional growth. For their part, universities must become vigilant against government policies and industry agreements that limit or delay the intellectual property researchers can disclose. These requirements, which are mounting daily, may well discourage or even impede the advancement of knowledge, which retards the efficient pursuit of scientific progress, and in turn slows innovation in industry.

The Partnership Rush

In the creative economy, ideas and intellectual capital have replaced natural resources and mechanical innovations as the raw material of economic growth. The university becomes more critical than ever as a provider of talent, knowledge, and innovation in the age of creative capitalism. It provides these resources largely by conducting and openly publishing research and by educating students. The university is empowered in this role by generating new discoveries that increase its eminence. In this way, academic research differs markedly from industry R&D, which is powered by the profit motive and takes place in an environment of secrecy.

In order to generate new discoveries and become better regarded, the university engages in a productive competition for the most revered academics. The presence of this top talent, in turn, attracts outstanding graduate students. They further enhance the university's reputation, helping to attract top undergraduates, and so on. The pursuit of eminence is reflected in contributions to new knowledge, typically embodied in academic publication.

Universities, like all institutions, require funding to pursue their objectives. There is a fundamental tension between the pursuit of excellence and the need for financial resources. Although industry funding does not necessarily hinder the quest for eminence, industry funds can, and increasingly do, come with restrictions, such as control over publishing or excessive secrecy requirements, which undermine the university's ability to establish academic prestige. This phenomenon is not new: At the turn of the century, chemistry and engineering departments were host to deep struggles between faculty who wanted to pursue industry-oriented research and those who wanted to conduct more pure science-driven research. Rapidly expanding federal research funding in the decades after World War II temporarily eclipsed that tension, but it is becoming more accentuated and widespread as knowledge becomes the primary source of economic advantage.

University ties to industry have grown enormously in recent times. Industry has become more involved in sponsored research, and universities have focused more on licensing their technology and creating spin-off companies to raise money. Between 1970 and 1997, for example, the share of industry funding of academic R&D rose sharply from 2.6 percent to 7.1 percent, according to the National Science Foundation (NSF). Patenting by academic institutions has grown exponentially. The top 100 research universities were awarded 177 patents in 1974, then 408 in 1984, and 1,486 in 1994. In 1997, the 158 universities surveyed by the Association of University Technology Managers applied for more than 6,000 patents. Universities granted roughly 3,000 licenses based on these patents to industry in 1998—up from 1,000 in 1991—generating roughly $500 million in royalty income.

A growing number of universities such as Carnegie Mellon University and the University of Texas at Austin have also become directly involved in the incubation of spin-off companies. Carnegie Mellon University hit the jackpot with its incubation of Lycos, the Internet search engine company; it made roughly $25 million on its initial equity stake in Lycos when the company went public. Other universities have joined in the startup gold rush, but this puts them in the venture capital game, a high-stakes contest where they don't necessarily belong. Boston University, for example, lost tens of millions of dollars on its ill-fated investment in Seragen. These activities do little to advance knowledge *per se* and certainly don't help attract top people. They instead tend to distract the university from its core missions of conducting research and generating talent. The region surrounding the university may not even benefit if it does not have the required infrastructure and environment to keep these companies in the area; Lycos moved to Boston because it needed high-level management and marketing people it could not find in Pittsburgh.

Joint university-industry research centers have also grown dramatically, and a lot of money is being spent on them. A 1990 Carnegie Mellon University study of 1,056 of these U.S. centers (those with more than $100,000 in funding and at least one active industry partner), conducted by Wesley Cohen, W. Richard Goe, and myself, showed that these centers had total funding in excess of $4.12 billion. And that was nine years ago. The centers involved 12,000 university faculty and 22,300 doctoral-level researchers—a considerable number.

In recent years, a debate has emerged over what motivates the university to pursue closer research ties with industry. The corporate manipulation view is that corporations seek to control relevant research for their own ends. In the academic entrepreneur view, university faculty and administrators act as entrepreneurs, cultivating opportunities for industry and public funding to advance their own agendas. The findings of our Carnegie Mellon survey support the academic entrepreneur thesis. Some 73 percent of the university-industry research centers indicated that the main impetus for their formation came from university faculty and administrators. Only 11 percent reported that their main impetus came from industry.

This university initiative did not occur in a vacuum, though. It was prompted by federal science and technology policy. More than half of all funding for university-industry research centers comes from government. Of the centers in our Carnegie Mellon survey, 86 percent received government support, 71 percent were established based on government support, and 40 percent reported that they could not continue without this support.

Three specific policies hastened the move toward university-industry research centers. The Economic Recovery Tax Act of 1981 extended industrial R&D tax breaks to research supported at universities. The Patent and Trademark Act of 1980, otherwise known as the Bayh-Dole Act, permitted universities to take patents and other intellectual property rights on products created under federally funded research and to assign or license those rights to others, frequently industrial corporations. The NSF established several programs that tied federal support to industry participation, such as the Engineering Research Centers, and Science and Technology Centers. Collectively, these initiatives also encouraged universities to seek closer research ties to business by creating the perception that future competition for federal funds would require demonstrated links to industry.

The rush to partner with industry has caused uncomfortable symptoms to arise. Industry is becoming more concerned with universities' overzealous pursuit of revenues from technology transfer, typically at the hands of technology transfer offices and intellectual property policies. Large firms are most upset that, even though they fund research up front, universities and their lawyers are forcing them into unfavorable negotiations over intellectual property when something of value emerges. Angered executives at a number of companies are taking the position that they will not fund research at universities that are too aggressive on intellectual property issues. One corporate vice president for industrial R&D recently summed up the sentiment of large companies, saying, "The university takes this money, then guts the relationship."

Smaller companies are concerned about time delays in getting research results, which occur because of protracted negotiations by university technology-transfer offices or attorneys over intellectual property rights. The deliberations slow the process of getting new technology into highly competitive markets, where success relies on commercializing innovations and products as soon as possible. Some of the nation's largest and most technology-intensive firms are beginning to worry aloud that increased industrial support for research is disrupting, distorting, and damaging the underlying educational and research missions of the university, retarding advances in basic science that underlie these firms' long-term futures.

Critics contend that growing ties to industry skew the academic research agenda from basic toward applied research. The evidence here is mixed. Studies by Diane Rahm and Robert Morgan at Washington University in St. Louis found a small empirical association between greater faculty involvement with industry and more applied research. Research by Harvard professor David Blumenthal and others showed that industry-supported research in biotechnology tended to be *short-term*. But NSF statistics show that, overall, the composition of academic R&D has remained relatively stable since 1980, with basic research at about 66 percent, although this is down from 77 percent in the early 1970s.

The larger and more pressing issue involves growing secrecy in academic research. Most commentators have posed this as an ethical issue, suggesting that increased secrecy contradicts the open dissemination of scientific knowledge. But the real problem is that secrecy threatens the efficient advancement of scientific frontiers. This is particularly true of so-called disclosure restrictions that govern what can be published and when. Over half of the centers in the Carnegie Mellon survey said that industry participants could force a delay in publication, and more than a third reported that industry could have information deleted from papers prior to publication.

Some have argued that the delays are relatively short and that the withheld information is of marginal importance in the big picture of science. But the evidence does not necessarily support this view. A survey by Blumenthal and collaborators indicated that 82 percent of companies require academic researchers to keep information confidential to allow for filing a patent application, which typically can take two to three months or more. Almost half (47 percent) of firms report that their agreements occasionally require universities to keep results confidential for even longer. The study concludes that participation with industry in the commercialization of research is "associated with both delays in publication and refusal to share research results upon request." Furthermore, in a survey by Rahm of more than 1,000 technology managers and faculty at the top 100 R&D-performing universities in the United States, 39 percent reported that firms place restriction on information-sharing by faculty. Some 79 percent of technology managers and 53 percent of faculty members reported that firms had asked that certain research findings be delayed or kept from publication.

These conditions also heighten the chances that new information will be restricted. A 1996 *Wall Street Journal* article reported that a major drug company suppressed findings of research it sponsored at the University of California San Francisco. The reason: The research found that cheaper drugs made by other manufacturers were therapeutically effective substitutes for its drug, Synthroid, which dominated the $600-million market for controlling hypothyroidism. The company disallowed publication of the research in a major scientific journal even though the article had already been accepted. In another arena, academic economists and officials at the National Institutes of Health have openly expressed concern that growing secrecy in biotechnology research may be holding back advances in that field.

Despite such troubles, universities continue to seek more industry funding, in large part because they need the money. According to Pennsylvania State University economist Irwin Feller, the most rapidly increasing source of academic research funding is the university itself. Universities increasingly believe that they must invest in internal research capabilities by funding centers and laboratories in order to compete for federal funds down the road. Since most schools are already strapped for cash and state legislatures are trimming budgets at state schools, more administrators are turning to licensing and other technology transfer vehicles as a last resort. Carnegie Mellon used the $25 million from its stake in Lycos to finance endowed chairs in computer science and the construction of a new building for computer science and multimedia research.

Spurring Regional Development

The role of the university as an engine for regional economic development has captured the fancy of business leaders, policymakers, and academics, and has led them astray. When they look at technology-based regions such as Silicon Valley in California and Route 128 around Boston, they conclude that the university has powered the economic development there. A theory of sorts has emerged that assumes that a linear pathway exists from university science and research, to commercial innovation, to an ever-expanding network of newly formed companies in the region.

This is a partial and mechanistic view of the way a university contributes to economic development. It is clear that Silicon Valley and Route 128 are not the only places in the United States where excellent universities are working on commercially important research. The real key is that communities surrounding universities must have the capability to absorb and exploit the science, innovation, and technologies that the university generates. In short, the university is a necessary, but not sufficient, condition for regional economic development.

Michael Fogarty and Amit Sinha have examined the outward flow of patented information from universities and have identified a simple but illuminating pattern: There is a significant flow of intellectual property from universities in older industrial regions, such as Detroit and Cleveland, to high-technology regions such as the greater Boston, San Francisco, and New York metropolitan areas. Their research suggests that even though new knowledge is generated in many places, it is only those regions that can absorb and apply those ideas that are able to turn them into economic wealth.

In addition to its role in incubating innovations and transferring commercial technology, the university plays an even broader and more fundamental role in the attraction and generation of talent—the creative people who work in, and are likely to form, entrepreneurial high-tech enterprises. The labor market for creative workers is different from the general labor market. Highly skilled people are highly mobile. They do not necessarily respond to monetary incentives alone; they want to be around other smart people. The university plays a magnetic role in the attraction of talent, supporting a classic increasing-returns phenomenon. Good people attract other good people, and places with lots of good people attract firms who want access to that talent, creating a self-reinforcing cycle of growth.

A key, and all too frequently neglected, role of the university in the creative economy is as a collector of talent—a growth pole that attracts eminent scientists and engineers, who then attract energetic graduate and undergraduate students, who create spin-off companies, all of which encourages companies to locate nearby. Still, the university is only one part of the system of attracting and keeping talent in an area. It is up to companies and other institutions in the region to put in place the opportunities and amenities required to make the region attractive to that talent in the long run. If the region does not have the opportunities, or if it lacks the amenities, the talent will leave.

Focus groups conducted with creative workers indicated that these talented people have many career options and that they can choose where they want to live and work. Generally speaking, they want to work in progressive environments, frequent upscale shops and cafes, enjoy museums and fine arts and outdoor activities, send their children to superior schools, and run into people, at all these places, from other advanced research labs and cutting-edge companies in their neighborhood. Researchers who do leave the university to start companies need quick access to venture capital, top management and marketing employees, and a pool of smart people from which to draw employees. They will not stick around the area if they can't find all these things. What's more, young graduates know they will probably change employers at least three times in 10 years, and they will not move to an area where they do not feel that enough quality employers exist to provide these opportunities. Stanford University didn't turn the Silicon Valley area into a high-tech powerhouse on its own; regional actors built the local infrastructure that this kind of creative economy requires. The same was true in Boston and, more recently, in Austin, Texas, where regional leaders undertook aggressive measures to create incubator facilities, venture capital, outdoor amenities, and the environmental quality that knowledge workers who participate in the creative economy demand.

It is important to note that this cycle has to not only be triggered by regional action, but also sustained by it. Over time, any university or region must be constantly repopulated with new talent. More so than industrial economies, leading universities and labor markets for knowledge workers are distinguished by high degrees of churning. What matters is the ability to replenish the talent stock. This is particularly true in advanced scientific and technical fields, where learned skills (such as engineering techniques) tend to depreciate rather quickly.

Regions that want to leverage this talent must make their areas attractive to this talent. In the industrial era, regions worked hard to attract factories that spewed out goods, paid taxes, and increased demand for other local businesses. Regional authorities built infrastructure and even offered financial inducements. But pressuring universities to develop more ties with local industry or expand technology transfer programs can have only a limited effect in the creative economy, since what it takes to build a truly vibrant regional economy is a harnessing of innovation and retention and attraction of the best talent the market has to offer.

The University as Talent Magnet

The new view of the university, as fueling the economy primarily through the attraction and creation of talent, as well as by generating innovations, has important implications for public policy. To date, federal, state, and local policy that encourages economic gain from universities has been organized as a giant *technology push* experiment. The logic is: If the university can just push more innovations out the door, those innovations will somehow magically turn into economic growth. But the economic effects of universities emanate in more subtle ways. Universities do not operate as simple engines of innovation. They are a crucial piece of the infrastructure of the creative economy, providing mechanisms for generating and harnessing talent. Once policymakers embrace this new view, they can begin to update or craft new policies that will improve the university's impact on the U.S. creative economy.

We do not have to stop promoting university-industry research or transferring university breakthroughs to the private sector, but we must support the university's role in the broader creation of talent.

At the national level, government must realize that the United States has to attract the world's best talent, and that a completely open university research system is needed to do so. It is probably time for a thoroughgoing review of the U.S. patent system and federal laws such as the Bayh-Dole Act, which incorporates a framework for protecting intellectual property based on the model of the university as an innovation engine. It must be reevaluated in light of the framework based on a university as a talent magnet.

Regional policymakers have to reduce the pressure on universities to expand technology transfer efforts in order to bolster the area's economy. They can no longer pass off this responsibility to university presidents. They have to step up themselves to ensure that the infrastructure that their region has to offer will be able to attract and retain top talent and absorb academic research results for commercial gain.

Meanwhile, business, academic, and policy leaders need to resolve the thorny issues arising as symptoms of bad current policy, such as disclosure restrictions that may be impeding the timely advancement of science, engineering, and commercial technology. Individual firms have clear and rational incentives to impose disclosure restrictions on work they fund, to ensure that their competitors do not get access. But as this kind of behavior multiplies, more and more scientific information of potential benefit to many facets of the economy is withheld from the public domain. This is a vexing problem that must be solved.

Universities, for their part, need to be more vigilant in managing this process. One solution that would not involve government at all would be for universities to take the lead in establishing shared and enforceable guidelines limiting disclosure restrictions. In doing so, universities will need to reconsider their more aggressive policies toward technology transfer, and particularly regarding the ownership of intellectual property.

As we move toward a creative economy, the university looms as a much larger source of economic raw material than in the past. If our country and its regions are really serious about building the capability to prosper in the creative economy, they will have to do much more than simply enhance the ability of the university to commercialize technology. They will have to create an infrastructure that is more conducive to talent. Here, policymakers can learn a great deal from the universities themselves, which within their walls have been creating environments conducive to talented and creative people for a very long time.

8
PLACE-MAKING AFTER 9/11
Rebuilding Lower Manhattan for the Creative Age

The great transformations in the factors driving contemporary urban success in America were already well in place before 2001. In September of that year, of course, a large portion of downtown Manhattan, home to some of the city's most creative workers and innovative firms, was destroyed by terrorists. While much of the debate swirling around how to rebuild what was there has focused on architecture and memorials, not as much has been said about what *type* of place the district will become. Will it simply be a newer version of what preceded it—a financial district that shuts down after business hours and continues to see many of its businesses slowly migrate to midtown and New Jersey? Or can it be something different, a place that harnesses the creative energies fueling contemporary urban innovation?

The tragedy of 9/11 had a huge effect on me. As a boy, I watched the Twin Towers being built from the bluff overlooking the meadowland in my hometown of North Arlington. I undertook the research for this chapter immediately in the wake of the tragic events of September 2001. I immediately called the Regional Plan Association and offered my assistance to their planning process for rebuilding the site of the former World Trade Center. I completed this project as a small personal contribution to that building process.

This chapter looks at the rebuilding of Lower Manhattan through the lens of my creativity-based theory of economic development. It begins from my premise that it would be counter-productive to use financial incentives to lure firms back into the district, or to try to use public funds to invest in whole new technology-based industrial sectors. In contrast, it emphasizes the development of broad quality-of-place amenities and lifestyle assets and the creation of a climate that can and will attract creative people of all types. It also emphasizes doing all of this in a way that is open to a diversity of both economic activity and people, and that invests in transit and other forms of connectivity that can link the region's evolving creative subcenters.

To get at these issues, I have applied the measures of regional dynamism discussed throughout this book to the New York Region: the High-Tech Index, which measures the relative size of a region's high-tech economy (in dollars of revenue) as a share of both the national high-tech total and the region's own overall economy; the Innovation Index, which measures patents granted in a region over the period 1990 to 1999, per 10,000 population; the Gay Index, which measures the over- or under-representation of coupled gay people in a region relative to the U.S. as a whole and therefore the region's relative degree of tolerance; and the Bohemian Index, which measures the concentration of professional artists, writers, and performers in a region relative to the national average. The overall Creativity Index is a composite of the first three measures, and hence a combined measure of the 3 T's, Technology, Talent, and Tolerance. Regions with a high Creativity Index are leading—or emerging—creative centers.

With this background in mind, let's take a look at where the Greater New York region stands. To do so, I compare the New York Consolidated Metropolitan Statistical Area to other large regions (CMSAs and MSAs) on my various indicators (see Tables 8.1 to 8.3). There are 49 regions in the United States with a population over one million. Generally speaking, the New York region stacks up well on the core measures of creativity.

New York as a Creative Region

The New York region has more than 2.5 million creative workers, far and away the most of any large U.S. region, as Table 8.1 shows. The

Table 8.1 Total Creative Employment

RANK	REGION	TOTAL CREATIVE WORKERS
1	New York	2,688,810
2	Los Angeles	1,984,700
3	Washington-Baltimore	1,458,580
4	Chicago	1,389,160
5	San Francisco	1,211,520
6	Philadelphia	927,090
7	Dallas-Fort Worth	825,390
8	Detroit	776,540
9	Boston	746,230
10	Houston	691,600
11	Atlanta	641,700
12	Minneapolis-St. Paul	578,520
13	Seattle	561,730
14	Denver	451,070
15	Miami	440,450

Table 8.2 The Creativity Index

CREATIVITY INDEX RANK	REGION	CREATIVITY INDEX SCORE
1	San Francisco	1057
2	Austin	1028
3	Boston	1015
4	San Diego	1015
5	Seattle	1008
6	Raleigh-Durham	996
7	Houston	980
8	Washington	964
9	New York	962
10	Dallas-Fort Worth	960
11	Minneapolis-St. Paul	960
12	Los Angeles	942
13	Atlanta	940
14	Denver	940
15	Chicago	935

New York region also ranks 9th overall on the Creativity Index, with a score of 962, as Table 8.2 shows.

The region scores consistently highly on the subcomponents of the Creativity Index, as Table 8.3 shows. This reinforces its status as a broadly creative region. It scores in the top 15 on three of the four core subcomponents of the Creativity Index—12th in Creative Class

Table 8.3 Creativity, Technology and Diversity

CREATIVITY INDEX RANK	REGION	CREATIVE CLASS	HIGH-TECH INDEX	INNOVATION	DIVERSITY (GAY INDEX)
1	San Francisco	34.8% (5)	8.81 (1)	134.3 (2)	2.01 (1)
2	Austin	36.4% (4)	2.71 (11)	125.7 (3)	1.19 (16)
3	Boston	38.0% (3)	7.18 (2)	69.4 (6)	1.04 (22)
4	San Diego	32.1% (15)	2.67 (12)	62.1 (7)	1.46 (3)
5	Seattle	32.7% (9)	5.24 (3)	40.1 (12)	1.32 (8)
6	Raleigh-Durham	38.2% (2)	2.48 (14)	79.0 (4)	1.00 (28)
7	Houston	32.5% (10)	1.86 (16)	36.6 (16)	1.2410)
8	Washington-Baltimore	38.4% (1)	4.83 (5)	25.9 (30)	1.22 (11)
9	New York	32.3% (12)	2.49 (13)	34.1 (24)	1.21 (14)
10	Dallas-Fort Worth	30.2% (23)	4.51 (6)	36.6 (17)	1.26 (9)
11	Minneapolis-St. Paul	33.9% (6)	0.80 (21)	73.5 (5)	0.97 (29)
12	Los Angeles	30.7% (20)	5.05 (4)	27.6 (29)	1.42 (4)
13	Atlanta	32.0% (16)	4.26 (7)	25.4 (31)	1.33 (7)
14	Denver	33.0% (8)	0.17 (38)	44.3 (10)	1.17 (18)
15	Chicago	32.2% (14)	3.06 (9)	33.2 (26)	1.02 (24)

concentration (with 32.3 percent), 13th on the High-Tech index, and 14th on the Gay Index. The New York region scores a respectable 24th on the Innovation index (measured as patents per population). Only two regions, San Francisco and Seattle, go four for four. Indeed, in terms of high-tech industry, the New York region scores higher than one might think. Its 13th place rank puts it ahead of the vaunted Raleigh-Durham Research Triangle, and far ahead of emerging high-tech areas like Denver and Minneapolis.

The Greater New York region also scores highly on another measure of creativity, the Bohemian Index. Though not part of the combined Creativity Index, it is, as noted previously, a potent indicator in its own right. New York CMSA ranks second out of 49 large regions on the Bohemian Index, behind only Nashville MSA—and New York's cultural scene is far more diverse. New York is one of just a few large regions—Boston, San Francisco, and Seattle are the others—ranking top-10 on both the economically-focused Creativity Index and the culturally-focused Bohemian Index.

As a whole, then, Greater New York is one of the nation's leading creative regions. It has evolved, and will continue to evolve, as a broadly

creative region of which financial services is but one important component. Given trends in the region's economy that indicate the decentral-
ization of financial functions away from Lower Manhattan (for
combined economic and security reasons), these findings further support the idea that strategic planning and investments should be undertaken in the context of a broader evolution of Lower Manhattan, away
from its strong specialization and historic concentration in financial
services, and toward a more broadly creative environment.

Compounding this, the New York region is emerging as the interlay
node in a broader East Coast Creative Corridor that stretches from
Boston to Washington, D.C. This corridor accounts for more than five
million creative workers, some 15 percent of the entire Creative Class.
In addition to New York at 9th, Boston ranks 3rd, Washington, D.C.,
ranks 8th, and Philadelphia ranks 17th on the Creativity Index. This
East Coast Creative Corridor does not yet have quite the concentrations of creative activity found in the West Coast corridor, which
stretches from Seattle through San Francisco and Los Angeles to San
Diego.

But the East Coast corridor with New York as its hub is larger, with
higher populations and more total creative workers, and it is more geo-
graphically compact; only 200 miles separate New York from Washington, D.C., or Boston, and much of this is connected by rail as well as by
air and highway links. The East Coast complex functions as a creative
meta-region more than the West Coast corridor does, and appears capable of functioning as one to a still greater extent.

It is important to recognize the role of New York in this meta-region
and to then undertake the rail, transit, and other investments that
strengthen and reinforce that role. That means placing a high priority
on inter-regional as well as intra-regional (high-speed) rail links
throughout the corridor connecting New York to creative complexes
from Boston to New Haven in the northeast as well as Princeton,
Philadelphia, Baltimore, and Washington, D.C., to the south. There are
likely to be considerable payoffs to envisioning New York as a critical
node in this broader creative complex and to undertaking strategic and
policy decisions that leverage and reinforce that role.

New York as a Multinodal Creative Center

But New York is not simply a node in a multistate corridor—it is internally dynamic as well. To get a better look at the internal composition of Greater New York, my research team and I developed our core creativity measures for the various sub-centers (or PMSAs) that make up the region. This analysis is based on a comparison of the 313 PMSAs nationwide for which reasonably comparable data are available.

Based on this, we found that the sub-centers that make up Greater New York appear as nodes in a network, each with its own mix of creative facets and strengths. The whole thrives because of its parts, and has the potential to thrive even more.

Table 8.4 presents the overall Creativity Index scores and Creative Class percentages for major New York subcenters. Briefly put:

- Six of the 11 sub-centers that comprise the Greater New York region break the 1,000 barrier on the Creativity Index. New York City, New Haven, Duchess County, Middlesex-Somerset-Hunterdon, Trenton, and Newark, once deemed the nation's poster child for urban decay. Long Island and Monmouth-Ocean are in the 900s. Only Newburgh even comes close to scoring in the lower half, out of 313 PMSAs nationally, on the Creativity Index.

Table 8.4 The Creative Class and Creativity Index for New York Subcenters

SUB-CENTER	CREATIVITY INDEX	CREATIVITY INDEX RANK	CREATIVE CLASS%	CREATIVE CLASS RANK
New York City *	1068	24	33.8%	20
Nassau-Suffolk	947	47	29.7%	84
New Haven-Meriden	1037	27	30.4%	61
Duchess County	1047	25	33.6%	22
Newburgh	662	134	25.8%	198
Bergen-Passaic	892	57	28.2%	127
Jersey City	826	76	28.9%	100
Newark	1094	14	31.7%	43
Middlesex-Somerset-Hunterdon	1094	14	35.3%	13
Monmouth-Ocean	915	53	29.6%	88
Trenton	1094	14	38.5%	6

*The New York City PMSA includes Westchester, Rockland and Putnam Counties.

- Six of the 11 subcenters also have Creative Class concentrations of 30 percent or more. There is an area of especially heavy concentration stretching from Newark through Middlesex and into Trenton, New Jersey. Trenton, with 38.5 percent of its workforce in the Creative Class, is among the nation's leaders. New York City and Duchess County also have above 30 percent of their workforces in the Creative Class occupations.
- New York City, with a score of 1068 on the Creativity Index, serves as the center and locational hub for this broad multinodal complex.

These are two of the most important creative economic outcomes. As Table 8.5 shows, the New York region contains vigorous pockets, or clusters, of high-tech industry and innovation.

- Two of the subcenters—New York City and Middlesex, New Jersey—rank in the top 10 out of 313 PMSAs nationwide on the High-Tech Index.
- Two others—Duchess County and Trenton, New Jersey—rank on the top ten on the Innovation Index.
- Three additional sub-centers—Newark, Nassau-Suffolk, and New Haven—score in the top 10 percent of high-tech regions, while Newark also does so on the Innovation Index.

Table 8.5 High-Tech and Innovation Indexes for New York Subcenters

SUB-CENTER	HIGH-TECH INDEX	HIGH-TECH RANK	INNOVATION INDEX	INNOVATION INDEX RANK
New York City	3.66	8	18.3	143
Nassau-Suffolk	1.41	28	27.3	100
New Haven-Meriden	1.40	29	41.2	51
Duchess County	0.25	71	131.4	7
Newburgh	0.01	216	23.7	117
Bergen-Passaic	0.51	51	36.6	58
Jersey City	0.07	111	11.8	201
Newark	2.42	21	55.9	28
Middlesex-Somerset-Hunterdon	3.64	9	93.28	13
Monmouth-Ocean	0.81	37	47.7	40
Trenton	0.29	65	98.4	10

- This suggests a reasonably powerful high-tech corridor stretching from New York City through Newark, Middlesex, and Trenton, New Jersey, and extending up into southwestern Connecticut as well. Again, New York City, and by extension Lower Manhattan, functions as the locational hub for this multinodal complex.

Tables 8.6 and 8.7 turn to a variety of demographic indicators of tolerance and openness to diversity. As we have seen, openness to diversity increases a region's capacity to attract creative people and generate creative economic outcomes.

The key findings:

- New York City and Jersey City score exceptionally high on the Gay Index.
- New York City scores extremely highly on the Bohemian Index. Trenton and Bergen-Passaic, New Jersey, also score in the top 10 percent of regions on this measure.

As Table 8.7 on the next page shows, New York City also ranks highly on the Melting Pot Index (which measures the percent foreign-born), as do Jersey City, Bergen-Passaic, and Newark. This New York-New Jersey corridor remains a magnet for new immigrants and a

Table 8.6 Gay and Bohemian Indexes for New York Subcenters

SUB-CENTER	GAY INDEX	GAY RANK	BOHEMIAN INDEX	BOHEMIAN RANK
New York	1.53	5	2.20	3
Nassau-Suffolk	0.87	85	1.07	69
New Haven-Meriden	0.93	66	0.95	110
Duchess County	0.82	97	NA	271
Newburgh	0.96	56	NA	268
Bergen-Passaic	0.79	116	1.33	30
Jersey City	1.51	6	1.18	46
Newark	0.95	58	0.98	95
Middlesex-Somerset-Hunterdon	0.79	115	1.05	74
Monmouth-Ocean	0.70	165	0.87	126
Trenton	0.92	69	1.39	21

Table 8.7 Melting Pot and Interracial Indexes for New York Subcenters

SUB-CENTER	MELTING POT	MELTING POT RANK	INTERRACIAL INDEX	INTERRACIAL RANK
New York	30.5%	6	3.7%	114
Nassau-Suffolk	12.7%	36	1.5%	212
New Haven-Meriden	9.1%	50	2.4%	159
Duchess County	NA	267	NA	286
Newburgh	NA	252	NA	134
Bergen-Passaic	21.1%	12	7.8%	43
Jersey City	35.4%	2	3.9%	107
Newark	18.0%	16	2.3%	164
Middlesex-Somerset-Hunterdon	14.5%	28	2.0%	181
Monmouth-Ocean	8.9%	51	2.0%	179
Trenton	10.7%	39	2.1%	176

cauldron for ethnic diversity. Surprisingly, none of the New York sub-centers score particularly highly on the Interracial Index, which measures the percentage of interracial couples in a given area.

In short, the New York subcenters score well in terms of tolerance and diversity, with a diversity corridor stretching roughly from New York City through Jersey City, Newark, and into Bergen and Passaic counties in New Jersey. Again, New York City, and by extension Lower Manhattan, serves as center and locational hub for this diversity complex.

As these statistics confirm, the Greater New York Region is a multinodal Creative Center. It scores highly in terms of overall creativity, has substantial pockets of the Creative Class, and also scores highly on high-tech and innovation as well as diversity. At the center of this is New York City and lower Manhattan, which function as the hub of a multinodal, multifaceted, and diverse creative complex.

These findings suggest a policy of improving the linkage between New York City and the other regional nodes in order to help develop the sub-centers. The findings from my indicators for the different sub-centers also provide clues as to which areas might be most important to connect to Downtown, in particular the existing high-tech corridor stretching from New York City through Newark, Middlesex, and Trenton, New Jersey extending north into New Haven, Connecticut.

Such connections would include high-bandwidth telecommunications along with more traditional transit infrastructure.

Clearly, both the New York economy and Lower Manhattan are part of a broader transformation of the U.S. economy, away from an older-style industrial economy. Lower Manhattan's economy will continue to diversify, most likely evolving in two parallel, intertwined roles: as a creative district in its own right, and as a key hub in the region's creative network.

Remaking Lower Manhattan

An increasing number of experts and policymakers have argued for remaking Lower Manhattan as a mixed-use, live-work-learn-play development with less high-rise financial concentration. This makes sense for several reasons. My research, conducted through focus groups and interviews, indicates that creative workers strongly prefer the mixed-use type of urban setting, both for living and working. They are drawn to stimulating and experiential creative environments. They gravitate to the indigenous street-level culture found in Soho, Greenwich Village, and parts of Brooklyn and Jersey. They look for places with visible signs of diversity—different races, ethnicities, sexual orientations, income levels, or lifestyles. Lower Manhattan, with its proximity to creative and ethnic communities, is already becoming a cauldron for this kind of diversity. And as Jane Jacobs argued in her landmark study of just such a neighborhood, the chance interplays and casual encounters that result are highly conducive to new creative enterprises, including those not foreseen or consciously cultivated by planners.

Downtown could even supplant Midtown as the region's "designated meeting place" for creative activities. One might say that Midtown currently plays this role by default, largely because it has more amenities and is easier to get to. But Midtown is a high-end business district and, more recently, with the transformation of Times Square, a corporate-entertainment district. While Lower Manhattan has been perceived as a specialized financial center, it has the advantage of being located virtually at the crossroads of the region's diverse creative centers—stretching from Soho and Tribeca into Greenwich Village, and across to Brooklyn on one side and Hoboken and Jersey City, with their thriving artistic and music communities, on the other. These places are adjacent and connected to Downtown more so than to Midtown. Moreover, Downtown has for decades been New York's cheaper business district, which by definition makes it open to a wider variety of economic and everyday uses. One key question: Can these advantages be leveraged to turn Downtown into the central creative node, by providing easier access and more amenities? Or would such improvements hike real estate prices so much that this advantage would be lost? In any event, Lower Manhattan has the strategic location and proximity that make it the natural creative hub for the region.

The key to Lower Manhattan lies in leveraging this trend, to make it as diverse and stimulating a district as it can be, connected to other creative centers, and a place of choice for the members of the Creative Class. I offer some modest suggestions for consideration—not as a list of musts or to-dos but in the spirit of stimulating creative thinking about such a strategy.

Instead of trying to pick winners, give ideas a place to breed.
Redevelopment efforts should not be tied to firm and specific incentives, but rather be broadly directed to supporting the underlying conditions for creativity, innovation, and entrepreneurship. In my view, it would be a mistake to try to transform the area into a high-tech center by betting the farm on any one new industry, such as biotechnology. Greater New York already has established clusters of high technology, such as in central New Jersey and around major scientific and medical centers. Also, planners should generally avoid or make only limited use of the practice of trying to pick winners, putting a great deal of resources into emerging industries or technologies that appear hot at the time. This has not been very successful in other regions in the past. Emerging fields may evolve more slowly, or in quite different directions, than anticipated. Spectacular growth can come from unexpected quarters like biotechnology in the 1980s. No one knows what the next big thing will be. The best general policy is to build a broadly creative environment, conducive to the formation and adoption of new ideas.

Think of a revitalized Downtown as an idea generator, and the urban subcenters as incubators. Real estate costs in the rebuilt area downtown will be too high for high-tech incubators or start-ups. But new enterprises conceived from the interplay and buzz of Lower Manhattan can take root in other parts of the city and region that offer lower-cost lofts or storefront space.

Meanwhile, other forms of technology-intensive business could flourish Downtown. In particular, it makes good sense to think of technology-based firms and industries that can build off, spin off from, and relate to the existing concentration of financial services. The financial services industry itself is evolving into a more creative sector. Mayor Michael Bloomberg is a classic example of a creative person who found a new niche in this turbulent industry, and built new enterprises by mixing technology with financial expertise. A multifaceted mixed-use environment that attracts more such people could be the best bet for ensuring that the financial services industry remains dynamic and adaptive. It also makes sense to consider design-intensive and highly creative professional services (such as architecture, advertising, engineering, and some computer services) and other sectors that would benefit from similar physical and intellectual environments.

Higher education offers many cards to play. As Chapter 7 showed, universities are valuable not only as technology generators but more importantly as talent magnets and breeders of diversity and tolerance. In all these ways, they act as a crucial infrastructure for the Creative Age. The New York region is blessed throughout with great research universities, superb colleges, and other such educational institutions. Huge numbers of faculty members, researchers, students, scholars, and intellectuals live in the region, particularly in areas bordering Lower Manhattan. It makes sense not only to bolster the research and higher-education presence here, but also to think of Lower Manhattan as a node in the multicenter higher-education network. Perhaps new forms of cooperation, joint programs, and alliances can take root Downtown. One direction to consider is the establishment of think tanks or institutes that are open to leading scholars and intellectuals and creative types who work in area institutions, live in the region, or both. This would create hubs of activity, synergize the creative contributions of many currently scattered actors, and help to forge a broad creative community throughout the region.

Quality of place is critical. It is important to consider Lower Manhattan as a center for consumption as well as production. As research by economist Edward Glaeser and sociologists Richard Lloyd and Terry Clark shows, the new city is becoming defined more and more as a city of consumption, experiences, lifestyle, and entertainment. Creative workers "increasingly act like tourists in their own city," write Lloyd and Clark. This means thinking of Lower Manhattan as a diverse, integrated live-work-learn-play community where the distinctions between these activities begin to blur. Retail is part of this strategy, as is lifestyle in general. Century 21 (the discount designer store) is already a major destination. Lower Manhattan is quite close to the rapidly expanding commercial corridor of Soho and adjacent neighborhoods. The area has seen substantial growth in hotels and visitors, particularly in Soho and Tribeca. The World Trade Center site is emerging as perhaps the New York region's most important tourist destination. Hotel infrastructure, lifestyle amenities, and shopping must be considered in any long-term development strategy.

It makes sense to invest in the quality of place that attracts creative workers, and also to enable the private sector to meet the amenity needs of this group by providing cafes and similar establishments. Members of the Creative Class prefer active, participatory forms of recreation and have come to expect them in urban centers. Along with street-level culture—the teeming blend of cafes, galleries, small music venues, and the like—where one can be a participant-observer, these workers enjoy active outdoor sports. This includes just-in-time outdoor exercise blended into a busy schedule: running at lunch hour, getting outdoors during a couple of spare hours on a Saturday or Sunday, biking to work, or taking the bus and then roller-blading home. If planning for Lower Manhattan can include provisions for such activities, such as parks and bicycle and foot lanes, it will be powerfully attractive not only to

Creative Class residents but to anyone who visits, uses, or lives in the area. The city must reconsider housing and zoning codes in light of the need for more (and more affordable) housing and conversion of extant buildings into residential or mixed-use facilities.

Many creative workers also like urban mixed-use live-work districts because they save time—just about everything you need is close by. In a creative economy, time is the only non-renewable resource and it is a precious one. As my research, and that of others, documents, professional Creative Class workers often suffer the most from the time crunch now afflicting all Americans. The old paradigm of urban high-rise office clusters for workers living in bedroom communities entails a long commute, and may eventually fade for that reason alone: Growing numbers of creative workers will no longer tolerate time-wasting commutes. In a massive national survey of information technology workers by *InformationWeek*, commuting distance was ranked among the most important job attributes by about 20% of respondents—outscoring items such as bonus opportunities and financial stability of the firm. Regions that find ways to cut their time overhead may well enjoy a competitive advantage in the future.

Connectivity Matters. Because of the need for people to save time, rebuilding and improving public transit must be a priority not only in and out of Lower Manhattan, but elsewhere. Creative growth *will* occur in *urban subcenters* and in far-flung corners of the region. Not everyone will live down the block from the office, or work at home, or do every meeting by teleconference. My focus groups and interviews indicate that Creative Class people value connectivity very highly, both as a way to get from point to point (on a 24/7 basis) but also as a way to save time. Intermodal travel may indeed grow, due to the ever-shifting nature of alliances among people and firms in a turbulent creative economy. This should include subway, rail, and water transit. Fast transit—and seated, hands-free transit, to allow work or rest while commuting —is of course the ideal.

For the past several years, the Downtown financial district has been expanding across the river into Jersey City and adjacent areas, where Goldman Sachs and other companies are building state-of-the-art facilities. Since 9/11, other companies have done the same. These trends provide a powerful opportunity to connect heretofore neglected, disconnected, or disadvantaged areas to the Lower Manhattan hub and to the Greater New York economy—I'm thinking here of Newark, Jersey City, Hoboken, Brooklyn, and surrounding areas. Cooperation throughout the Tri-state region is critical to rebuilding Lower Manhattan. This move will require new forms of regional partnering, including perhaps a commitment to eliminate the use of financial incentives to lure firms across state boundaries, to create cooperative economic development strategies and efforts, and to support shared regional revenue streams for major infrastructure and related investments.

A New Convergence Point? Lower Manhattan's central location in the region raises some intriguing possibilities as to its future business role. Could it become a designated meeting point, where people from various nodes in the network converge as needed or to conduct specific types of face-to-face business regularly? What kinds of facilities might this function require; what planning measures would support it? Here again, the key is Lower Manhattan's role as idea generator and Creative Hub.

New York in the Long View

The Greater New York economy is among the most dynamic in world history. The region's economy has evolved and remade itself numerous times over the centuries, and Lower Manhattan has consistently been a hub for these major economic transformations. In precolonial times, the region evolved into a major center for trade and commerce. By the eighteenth and nineteenth centuries it became a major center for manufacturing innovation, technology, and industrial production. With the onset of the twentieth century—and the coming of the great organizational age—the region's economy evolved once again into a center for corporate headquarters, high-level business services, and especially finance.

During each of these epochs, sweeping transformations in the region's economy have registered themselves in equally sweeping changes in the region's physical landscape and built environment. Nowhere has this been more evident than in Lower Manhattan, which has evolved from a trading center, to a manufacturing center, to the physical apex of the organizational age, and ultimately to the world's leading financial center. In the past, the region, and particularly its physical hub, has become a trendsetter for the growth and development of each new epoch in economic history. New York, it seems, has always been a key incubator of the ideas, technologies, organizational processes, and talent that define each new age. Over time, functions of the previous age decentralize from the urban core to make way for the new, as agriculture and manufacturing once did, and as large organizations and their functions have been doing more recently. The process appears to be occurring again today.

The potential for Lower Manhattan and the region is tremendous. New York has the opportunity, out of its tragedy, to become the paragon of the twenty-first century Creative Center. The city has led the way into previous ages, and has been the world capital of the organizational age. It has made a marvelous transition, thus far, to rank among the early pace setters in the creative age—which is not easy, as many great cities (and societies) fall by the wayside when the requirements for greatness change.

But more challenges lie ahead as the creative age unfolds. One fork looming in the road, for instance, is this: Economic and social divides have been growing throughout America. They can continue to grow, or vastly more people can be integrated into the creative economy—so that the masses of people, not just 30 percent of the workforce, enjoy the rewards of exercising their creativity at work. That would be a truly humane and a truly productive economy. What steps are required to take such a path? There is no better place than New York to find out.

9
OPEN QUESTIONS

In speeches across the country and the globe, I'm often asked the following question: In the time since *The Rise of the Creative Class* was originally published, what have you learned? The short answer is: a lot. But I'll briefly outline what I see as the *most* important issues confronting the emergence of the creative economy and hindering the rise of a more fully creative society that enhances and validates a broader range of human potential.

First and foremost, though the creative economy generates tremendous innovative, wealth-creating, and productive promise, left to its own devices it will neither realize that promise nor solve the myriad of social problems facing us today. Perhaps the most salient of what I consider the *externalities* of the creative age has to do with rising social and economic inequality. Less than a third of the workforce—the creative class—is employed in the creative sector of the economy. That means two thirds are not. Even more discouragingly, inequality is considerably worse in leading creative regions. Kevin Stolarick's Inequality Index compares the wages of creative sector workers to those in the manufacturing sectors (see my article "The New American Dream," *Washington Monthly* March 2003). Our findings clearly indicate that inequality is highest in places like San Francisco, the North Carolina Research

Triangle, Washington, D.C., and Austin. And, far from inequality being the only creative-age social concern, the creative economy generates other related externalities as well:

- **Housing affordability:** As the creative economy takes root in places like Boston and New York, it generates tremendous pressure on housing prices, both forcing artists and other creative people out of their communities and further exacerbating social and economic inequality between the haves and the have-nots of the creative economy.
- **Uneven regional development:** The creative economy generates overlapping economic and demographic trends that have combined to worsen regionally uneven development as pronounced as anything we've seen since the Civil War.
- **Sprawl and ecological decay:** The success of the creative economy produces development pressure that threatens the environment and stable ecosystems. This, in turn, undermines many of the natural features and amenities that made these places attractive in the first place.
- **Mounting stress and anxiety:** With the elimination of larger institutional and social support structures, the creative economy downloads stress and anxiety directly onto individuals. My preliminary findings with the psychiatric researchers Kenneth Thompson and Roberto Figueroa show that stress and anxiety is markedly higher—across all income and class groups—in regions with high Creativity Index scores.
- **Political polarization:** The creative economy is giving rise to pronounced political and social polarization—a demographic sorting process that separates people by economic position, cultural outlook, and political orientation. This *big sort* is further aggravated by the perception among many that key elements of the creative class are arrogant, hedonistic, and self-indulgent. The fissure runs deep through the very structure of American society, and makes it exceedingly difficult to generate coherent and forward-looking responses to the problems and challenges posed by the *global* creative economy.

Related to this last point, it is becoming increasingly clear how truly global the creative economy is. This is the subject I address in *The Flight of the Creative Class* (HarperBusiness 2005). Although many assume the United States to have an unbeatable edge, its position is more tenuous than commonly thought. But the United States certainly has many assets with which to compete. Over the past century, this country built the most powerful and dynamic economy in the world. It did so by fostering entire new industrial sectors, by maintaining a free and open society, by investing in scientific and cultural creativity, and, most of all, by drawing energetic and intelligent people from all over the world to its shores.

The key element of global competition is no longer trade of goods and services or flows of capital, but the ability to, on the one hand, harness the creative energy of a country's domestic population, and, on the other, to attract creative people from around the globe. Regions like Toronto and Vancouver in Canada, and Sydney and Melbourne in Australia, already compete effectively with leading U.S. creative centers, according to recent studies. European regions from Dublin and London to Helsinki, Amsterdam, and Copenhagen also do well. The United States, on the other hand, actually appears to have thrown the gearshift in reverse, cutting spending on research, education, and arts and culture, even as we restrict the influx of scientific information and of foreign-born scientists and engineers. The ability to attract people is a dynamic and sensitive process. New centers of the global creative economy can emerge rapidly; established players can lose position. Look how quickly regions like Austin or Seattle rose to the top of the pack among U.S. regions. The same thing can happen—and *is* happening—globally.

Furthermore, the rise of the creative economy is ushering in a transformation of social and cultural values throughout the world. Ronald Inglehart of the University of Michigan describes the process as a swing from an older, traditional set of values, focused on nuclear families and material gain, to an emphasis on "post-materialist" values, which revolve around quality of life, self-expression, and personal freedom. And while other countries have evolved more gradually from traditional to post-materialist values, the United States has cleaved in half. Some regions of the country are increasingly traditional—dominated by older-style industries, family values, slow growth, and rising anger. Other regions are more post-materialist and cosmopolitan—younger, hipper, faster-moving, and wealthier, and, in the eyes of many, increasingly shallow, self-absorbed, and hedonistic.

The people in these two different nations read different newspapers, watch different television shows, vote for different leaders, go about their work differently, and hold mutually incompatible views on almost every conceivable subject. Each side increasingly sees itself as the repository of the nation's best and truest self, and the other side as a hypocritical minority trying to impose its values on the rest of the country. If allowed to proceed unchecked, this process will result in a nation that is divided not only economically, but also culturally, socially, and politically. As mentioned above, this divide makes it virtually impossible for the United States to address critical economic and social issues with anything resembling a united front. What's more, it also means that intolerance has a considerable political base, making it harder still for the United States to remain the kind of place that is attractive to people from around the world.

Perhaps most importantly, lasting competitive advantage in the creative age will not simply amass in those countries and regions that can generate the most creative, innovative, or entrepreneurial output. For the key factor is not just innovative or creative capacity but also absorptive capacity. The nations and regions that will be most able to absorb will be those that are both open to diversity and also capable of internalizing the aforementioned externalities that the creative economy gives rise to. It will no longer be sufficient to incubate new creative industries or generate more creative people. A key factor in the ability to develop a creative economy and society will turn on the ability of regions and nations to cope with problems like income inequality, housing affordability, uneven development, and underutilized human potential in new and innovative ways.

Here, a historical analogy may be helpful. The rise of mass production industry during the late nineteenth and early twentieth centuries ushered in a period of incredible innovation, productivity improvement, and wealth creation. New industries were formed: railroad, steel, automobile, chemical, and others. But the returns on that increased productivity were highly unequal, accruing mainly to robber barons and their ilk. Manufacturing workers made little money and toiled long hours in deplorable—and often fatal—conditions. Cities were filthy and filled with smoke. Refuse flowed down streets, and ecological and public health nightmares abounded.

The full potential of the nascent industrial age required the development of a much more broadly based industrial society in which great masses of people could participate. This industrial society did not emerge on its own, but was spurred into existence by a series of policy interventions that gradually evolved and were institutionalized over the period stretching from the Great Depression and New Deal years into the immediate post-World War II era.

Part of the solution rested on the Keynesian nature of these interventions: the fact that they increased wages, spurred demand, and thus also spurred the growth and development of key industrial sectors. These programs encouraged the development of key mass production industries, from cars to appliances, by expanding the availability of home mortgages, investing in the development of a large-scale interstate highway system, expanding higher education, and increasing investments in research and development, among other things. But these policies and approaches also dealt effectively with the externalities of the unmediated industrial economy during its so-called *gilded age.*

And, amazingly, they did so in a way that did not stoke the fires of class warfare. In sharp contrast to many European nations, these programs actually brought capital and labor closer together, by encouraging the development of mass production unions, by linking wage increases to productivity gains, by improving health and safety in the workplace, and by creating social security for older people and basic social welfare service for the truly needy. This system thus squared the circle, driving the expansion of the industrial economy by allowing many more people (read: political and socioeconomic constituencies) to benefit from it, while simultaneously addressing a whole range of its negative externalities.

It may well be that a new group of regions and countries have an advantage in addressing the two horns of the new, modern-day economic dilemma. This advantage comes not from any preordained plan, but from the gradually evolved capability to cope with the externalities of the creative economy. Certainly, the United States has considerable assets with which to compete, but its political culture and current populace polarization leave it incapable of dealing with these externalities. Consequently, we find ourselves beset by the institutional rigidities of the sort that the late economist Mancur Olson identified as trapping established powers and ushering in their stagnation and decline.

So where to look? My sense is that it is a mistake to look toward countries like India and China to emerge as the only new dominant powers in this age. Rather, history seems, in this case, to be smiling upon a series of smaller, more nimble countries that have well-established mechanisms for social cohesion and are able both to mobilize their own creative energy from all segments of society, and to compete effectively for global talent. Although this age is just emerging and it is far too early to predict with any precision which nations will enjoy long-run economic advantage, in my opinion, the leading candidates include countries such as Canada, Sweden, Finland, Australia, and New Zealand, all of which score highly on all 3 T's of economic development: Technology, Talent, and Tolerance. These countries may have inherited the broad systems for generating social cohesion, the open-minded and tolerant values, and the capability not just to spur innovation and creativity, but to respond to and to internalize the tensions and externalities the creative economy implies.

Understanding this process of adaptation and crafting the social infrastructures that support and enable it are the critical open questions of our age. They are also the questions that my ongoing research and my next book deal with, and they deserve much more research from any and all interested parties—not just as an intellectual project, but in order that we may develop future models of social organization that better align economic development with the further development of *all* human potential. And the urban centers constantly undergoing social and economic transformations all around us provide compelling laboratories in which to continue the search for good ideas, better questions, and the best solutions.

APPENDIX

Rankings of Top 50 Metropolitan Areas by Various Indices

Rankings

REGION	TECH-POLE	COMPOSITE DIVERSITY	GAY INDEX	TECH-GROWTH INDEX	MELTING POT INDEX	BOHEMIAN INDEX	TALENT INDEX
San Francisco	1	2	1	10	4	8	3
Boston	2	6	8	36	9	9	2
Seattle	3	5	6	20	15	1	6
Washington	4	3	2	24	10	6	1
Dallas	5	15	19	9	16	15	10
Los Angeles	6	1	7	50	2	2	23
Chicago	7	11	15	13	7	20	13
Atlanta	8	14	4	5	31	13	5
Phoenix	9	21	22	3	21	24	35
New York	10	4	14	37	3	3	9
Philadelphia	11	32	36	27	25	35	20
San Diego	12	7	5	25	6	18	14
Denver	13	17	10	8	29	14	7
Austin	14	8	3	1	19	10	4
Houston	15	18	21	7	8	30	12
Portland	16	16	23	2	23	5	17
Indianapolis	17	40	34	40	44	34	31
Kansas City	18	34	35	11	42	22	24
Minneapolis	19	19	17	29	35	7	8
St. Louis	20	49	45	45	43	38	36

Rankings (*continued*)

REGION	TECH-POLE	COMPOSITE DIVERSITY	GAY INDEX	TECH-GROWTH INDEX	MELTING POT INDEX	BOHEMIAN INDEX	TALENT INDEX
Orlando	21	9	11	38	17	12	32
Sacramento	22	20	9	6	14	39	22
Detroit	23	26	44	33	20	25	48
San Antonio	24	31	32	4	12	50	40
Pittsburgh	25	46	39	26	37	46	39
West Palm Beach	26	13	16	34	11	16	33
Tampa	27	23	18	18	18	32	49
Columbus	28	29	25	28	38	29	21
Salt Lake City	29	28	41	19	28	23	25
Birmingham	30	50	49	35	50	42	38
Baltimore	31	38	31	44	33	44	18
Cincinnati	32	33	38	46	40	19	28
Charlotte	33	45	43	12	41	36	37
Dayton	34	41	26	39	45	43	43
Milwaukee	35	35	40	43	34	28	30
Cleveland	36	43	47	49	22	47	42
Miami	37	10	12	30	1	27	46
Rochester	38	22	13	31	24	31	19
Albany	39	36	30	41	30	45	15
Nashville	40	25	28	17	47	4	29
Greensboro	41	42	46	14	48	21	41
Oklahoma City	42	39	27	42	36	49	27
Las Vegas	43	24	48	21	13	11	50
Norfolk	44	37	37	15	32	37	45
Richmond	45	30	29	22	39	26	11
Buffalo	46	48	50	48	27	48	44
New Orleans	47	27	24	32	26	41	34
Honolulu	48	12	20	47	5	17	16
Memphis	49	44	33	23	46	40	26
Louisville	50	47	42	16	49	33	47

Statistics

Correlations utilized both a Pearson and a Spearman rank order correlation. The Pearson statistic measures the correlation between the values of two variables while the Spearman statistic measures the correlation between the relative rankings of the two variables. As such, the Spearman correlation tends to be less influenced by outliers in the data. All regression analysis utilized Ordinary Least Squares estimation techniques:

Correlation Analysis

Pearson Correlations Between Milken Tech-Pole and Growth Measures with Talent and Diversity Measures.[a]

	HIGH-TECH GROWTH	% COLLEGE GRADUATES	COMPOSITE DIVERSITY INDEX	BOHO INDEX	% FOREIGN BORN	GAY INDEX
Milken Tech-Pole	0.23 (0.10)	0.72 (0.001) 0.68 (0.001)	0.62 (0.001)	0.43 (0.002)	0.77 (0.001)	
High-Tech Growth		0.25 (0.08)	0.27 (0.06)	0.19 (0.19)	20.04 (0.78)	0.31 (0.03)

[a]Significance level shown in parenthesis. Bold cells are significant at 0.10 level or higher.

Spearman Rank Order Correlations Between Milken Tech-Pole and Growth Measures with Talent and Diversity Measures.[a]

	HIGH-TECH GROWTH	% COLLEGE GRADUATES	COMPOSITE DIVERSITY INDEX	BOHO INDEX	% FOREIGN BORN	GAY INDEX
Milken Tech-Pole	0.30 (0.03)	0.60 (0.001)	0.63 (0.001)	0.54 (0.001)	0.48 (0.001)	0.60 (0.001)
High-Tech Growth		0.20 (0.15)	0.23 (0.10)	0.24 (0.09)	0.07 (0.63)	0.26 (0.07)

[a]Significance level shown in parenthesis. Bold cells are significant at 0.10 level or higher.

Regression Analysis

OLS Estimation of the effects of various metropolitan area traits on the Milken Tech-Pole Index and Ranking.[a]

INDEPENDENT VARIABLES:	(1) DEPENDENT VARIABLE: MILKEN TECH-POLE	(2) DEPENDENT VARIABLE: MILKEN TECH-POLE RANKING	(3) DEPENDENT VARIABLE: MILKEN TECH-POLE	(4) DEPENDENT VARIABLE: MILKEN TECH-POLE
% College graduates	27.2* (7.25)	1.9* (5.46)		21.5* (4.99)
Bohemian Index			4.4* (5.43)	2.3** (2.90)
R-squared	0.52	0.38	0.38	0.59
N = 50				

  [a] Absolute value of t-statistics are shown in parentheses.
  * Significance < 0.001 level.
  ** Significance < 0.01 level.

OLS Estimation of the effects of various metropolitan area traits (measured in 1990) on high-technology growth from 1990 to 1998.[a]

INDEPENDENT VARIABLES:	DEPENDENT VARIABLE: HIGH-TECH GROWTH	
Composite diversity index	0.005*** (2.91)	—
Gay Index		0.15* (1.70)
% College Graduate	−0.41 (0.29)	−0.24 (0.15)
% Foreign Born		−0.28 (0.34)
Bohemian Index		0.26 (1.23)
Culture	−.00002 (0.27)	−0.00005 (0.69)
Recreation	−0.0002** (2.56)	−0.0001 (1.54)
Climate	−0.0001 (0.27)	−0.0004 (1.13)
Population	0.00 (0.80)	0.00 (0.001)
R-squared	0.32	0.28
N = 50		

  [a] Absolute value of t-statistics are shown in parentheses.
  * Significance < 0.10 level.
  ** Significance < 0.05 level.
  *** Significance < 0.01 level.

NOTES

Chapter 2

1. Kevin Kelley, *New Rules for the New Economy*, 1998, 94–5.
2. Robert Park, E. Burgess, and R. McKenzie, *The City* (Chicago: University of Chicago Press, 1925). Jane, Jacobs, *The Death and Life of Great American Cities* (New York, Random House, 1961). *The Economy of Cities* (New York: Random House, 1969); *Cities and the Wealth of Nations* (New York: Random House, 1984). Wilbur Thompson *A Preface to Urban Economics* (Baltimore: The Johns Hopkins University Press, 1965). Edwin Ullman "Regional Development and the Geography of Concentration," *Papers and Proceedings of the Regional Science Association*, 4, 1958, 179–98.
3. Michael Porter, "Clusters and the New Economics of Competition," *Harvard Business Review*, November-December 1998; "Location, Clusters, and Company Strategy," in Gordon Clark, Meric Gertler, and Maryann Feldman (eds.), *Oxford Handbook of Economic Geography* (Oxford: Oxford University Press, 2000). "Location, Competition and Economic Development: Local Clusters in a Global Economy," *Economic Development Quarterly*, 14, 1, February 2000, 15–34.
4. Maryann Feldman, "Location and Innovation: The New Economic Geography of Innovation, Spillovers, and Agglomeration" in Gordon Clark, Meric Gertler, and Maryann Feldman (eds.), *The Oxford Handbook of Economic Geography* (Oxford: Oxford University Press, 2000). Adam Jaffe, "Real Affects of Academic Research," *American Economic Review*, 79, 5, 1989; David Audretsch and Maryann Feldman, "R&D Spillovers and the Geography of Innovation and Production," *American Economic Review*, 86, 3, 1996; David Audretsch, "Agglomeration and the location of innovative activity," *Oxford Review of Economic Policy*, 14, 2, 1998, 18–30.
5. Robert Putnam, *Bowling Alone: The Collapse and Revival of American Community* (New York: Simon and Schuster, 2000).
6. Putnam, *Bowling Alone*. Also see Putnam, "The Prosperous Community," *The American Prospect*, Spring 1993; and, "The Strange Disappearance of Civic America," *The American Prospect*, Winter 1996.
7. For example, Christine Stansell, *American Moderns: Bohemian New York and the Creation of a New Century* (New York: Metropolitan Books, 2000).
8. Mancur Olson, *The Rise and Decline of Nations: Economic Growth, Stagflation, and Social Rigidities* (New Haven, CT: Yale University Press, 1986). *The Logic of Collective Action: Public Goods and the Theory of Groups* (Cambridge, MA: Harvard University Press, 1971).

9. Jane Jacobs, *Cities and the Wealth of Nations* (New York: Random House, 1984).

10. Robert Jucas, Jr., "On the Mechanics of Economic Development," *Journal of Monetary Economics*, 22, 1988, 38–9.

11. Edward Glaeser, "Are Cities Dying?" *Journal of Economic Perspectives*, 12, 1998, 139–160. The human capital literature has grown large; other important contributions include Glaeser, "The New Economics of Urban and Regional Growth," in Gordon Clark, Meric Gertler, and Maryann Feldmen (eds.), *The Oxford Handbook of Economic Geography* (Oxford: Oxford University Press, 2000), 83–98. James E. Rauch, "Productivity Gains from Geographic Concentrations of Human Capital: Evidence from Cities," *Journal of Urban Economics*, 34, 1993, 380–400. Curtis Simon, "Human Capital and Metropolitan Employment Growth," *Journal of Urban Economics*, 43, 1998, 223–243; Curtis Simon and Clark Nardinelli, "The Talk of the Town: Human Capital, Information and the Growth of English Cities, 1861–1961." *Explorations in Economic History*, 33, 3, 1996, 384–413. Vijay K. Mathur, "Human Capital-Based Strategy for Regional Economic Development," *Economic Development Quarterly*, 13/3, 1999, 203–216.

12. Spencer Glendon, "Urban Life Cycles," (Cambridge, MA: Harvard University, Department of Economics, unpublished working paper, November 1998).

13. The correlation between the Creative Class and innovation is 0.34, high-tech industry (0.38,) and talent (0.64): all are significant. The correlation between it and employment growth (0.03) are insignificant.

14. The high-tech leaders are San Francisco, Boston, Seattle, Los Angeles, and Washington, D.C., while the innovation leaders are Rochester, San Francisco, Austin, Boston, and the Research Triangle. The correlation between the Talent Index and the Creative Class is 0.64, which is understandable because these occupations require high levels of education. The correlation between the Talent Index and the Working Class is 20.45. Both are significant. The point of these correlations is not that talent is more associated with certain kinds of occupations, which should be obvious, but to again stress the geographic sorting and balkanization of American regions by occupation, human capital, and other factors. Fifteen of the top 20 Talent regions number among the top 20 high-tech regions while 14 of the top 20 Talent regions rank among the top 20 most innovative regions. The statistical correlations between these two factors are again uniformly high and significant. The Pearson correlation between the Milken Tech-Pole and the Talent Index is 0.4; the Spearman rank order correlation was 0.61. The Pearson correlation between Innovation and population with a college degree is 0.45; the Spearman correlation is 0.55.

15. John M. Quigley, "Urban Diversity and Economic Growth," *Journal of Economic Perspectives*, 12, 2, Spring 1998, 127–138.

16. Jane Jacobs, *The Death and Life of Great American Cities* (New York: Random House, 1961). *The Economy of Cities* (New York: Random House, 1969). *Cities and the Wealth of Nations* (New York: Random House, 1984). Also see A. E. Andersson, "Creativity and Regional Development," *Papers of the Regional Science Association*, 56, 1985, 5–20. Pierre Desrochers, "Diversity, Human Creativity, and Technological Innovation," *Growth and Change*, 32, 2001.

17. Pascal Zachary, *The Global Me, New Cosmopolitans and the Competitive Edge: Picking Globalism's Winners and Losers* (New York: Perseus Books Group, Public Affairs, 2000).

18. The correlation between the Melting Pot Index and Tech-Pole Index is 0.26 and significant. For patents it is 0.007 and insignificant. The correlation with population growth is 0.28 and significant, while for employment growth it is 0.04 and insignificant.

19. The correlation between the Creative Class and the Melting Pot Index (0.10) is insignificant as is that between Talent and the Melting Pot Index (.08).

20. The Pearson correlation between the 1990 Gay Index and the Tech-Pole Index is 0.57, and it is 0.48 using the 2000 Gay Index. Both are significant at the 0.001 level. The Pearson correlation between the 1990 Gay Index and technological growth is 0.17, and it is 0.16 using the 2000 Gay Index. Again, both are significant at the 0.001 level. The results were similar when we ran the analysis using the Progressive Policy Institute's New Economy Index for the 46 for which we could match the data.

21. The Growth Index measures change in high-tech output within metropolitan areas from 1990 to 1998 relative to national change in output during the same period.

22. Bill Bishop, "Technology and Tolerance: Austin Hallmarks," *Austin American-Statesman*, June 25, 2000.

23. Bohemians are positively correlated with high-tech industry (0.38), with population growth (0.28), and with employment growth (0.23.) All are significant at the 0.001 level.

24. Alone, the Bohemian Index can explain nearly 38 percent of the variation in high-tech concentration. Together, the Bohemian Index and the Talent Index account for nearly 60 percent of the high-tech concentration measure.

25. Robert Cushing, "Creative Capital, Diversity and Urban Growth," (Austin Texas, December 2001, unpublished paper).

Chapter 3

1. Peter Drucker, *The Post-Capitalist Society* (New York: Harper Business, 1993); and Ikujiro Nonaka and Hirotaka Takeuchi, *The Knowledge Creating Company* (New York: University Press, 1995).

2. Richard Florida, "Toward the Learning Region," *Futures: The Journal of Forecasting and Planning*, 27, 5 June: 1995, 527–36.

3. Ross DeVol, *America's High Technology Economy: Growth, Development, and Risks for Metropolitan Areas* (Milken Institute: 1999).

4. Tim W. Ferguson, "Sun, Fun, and Ph.D.s, Too," *Forbes*, May 30, 1999, 220.

5. *Yahoo! Internet Life* magazine, www.zdnet.com/yil/content/mag/9803

6. The data for creative workers is based on data for SIC 737. It is adapted from County Business Patterns. Data are shown for X of 35 benchmark regions.

7. Data on entrepreneurship are from David Birch, Anne Haggerty, and William Parsons, "Entrepreneurial Hot Spots: The Best Places in American to Start and Grow a Company," *Cognetics* (1999).

8. See Michael Porter and Claas van der Linde, "Toward a New Conception of the Environment-Competitiveness Relationship," *Journal of Economic Perspectives*, 9/1, 1995, 97–118; Michael Porter and Claas van der Linde, "Green and Competitive: Ending the Stalemate," *Harvard Business Review*, 1995, 120–134; Richard Florida, "Lean and Green: The Move to Environmentally Conscious Manufacturing," *California Management Review*, 39/1, 1996, 80–105.

9. Richard Florida and Tracy Gordon, *Regional Environmental Performance and Sustainability: A Review and Assessment of Indicator Projects*, Environmental City Network and Sustainable Pittsburgh, 1999; and Dave McGovern, "America's Best Walking Towns," *The Walking Magazine*, May/June 1998, 55.

10. Paul Gottlieb, "Amenities as an Economic Development Tool: Is There Enough Evidence?," *Economic Development Quarterly*, Vol. 8, No. 3, August 1994, 270–285.

11. The data on air and water quality are adapted from the rankings provided in from *Money Magazine*. The data on sprawl are from the Sierra Club.

12. See *Next Century Economy: Sustaining the Austin Region's Economic Advantage in the 21st Century* (Greater Austin Chamber of Commerce: 1998).

13. See Robert Lucas, "On the Mechanics of Economic Development," *Journal of Monetary Economics,* 22, (1988), 3–42. As Glaeser notes, the intellectual heritage of his position hearkens back to Alfred Marshall, *The Principles of Economics* (London: Macmillan, 1890) and Jane Jacobs, *The Life and Death of Great American Cities* (New York: Random House, 1961), and *The Economy of Cities* (New York: Random House, 1968).

14. Louis Tornatzky, Denis Gray, Stephanie Tarant, and Julie Howe, *Where Have All the Students Gone? Interstate Migration of Recent Science and Engineering Graduates* (Southern Technology Council, 1998).

15. The arts and culture measure is based on data adapted from *Money Magazine.*

16. The measure for professional sports is adapted from *Money Magazine.*

17. Data on the education level and knowledge intensity of the population are from the Public Use Microdata Sample of the U.S. Census. The diversity index is from Gates et al. (2000). Median house value is from the U.S. Census (it is expected that higher-median house values reflect higher levels of amenities). The culture, recreation, and climate measures are adapted from the *Places Rated Almanac.* The culture measure is a composite of radio broadcasts of classical music, public televisions stations, art museums and galleries, and arts and musical performances. The recreation measure includes restaurants, public golf courses, bowling lanes, zoos, and aquariums, family theme parks, automobile race tracks, pari-mutuel betting, professional and college sports teams, miles of coast line and inland water, and national parks.

18. KPMG/CATA Alliance, High Technology Labour Survey: Attracting and Retaining High Technology Workers (KPMG, June 5, 1998).

Chapter 4

1. Paul Romer, "Endogenous Technological Change." *Journal of Political Economy* 98, 5, 1990: S71–S102.

2. Jane Jacobs, *The Death and Life of Great American Cities* (New York: Random House, 1961).

3. Edwin Ullman, "Regional Development and the Geography of Concentration," *Papers and Proceedings of the Regional Science Association,* 4, 1958: 179–98.

4. Robert Lucas, Jr., "On the Mechanics of Economic Development," *Journal of Monetary Economics,* 22, 1988: 1–42. See also research by Edward Glaeser, "Are Cities Dying?," *Journal of Economic Perspectives,* 12, 1998: 139–60; "The New Economics of Urban and Regional Growth," In *The Oxford Handbook of Economic Geography,* ed. Gordon Clark, Meric Gertler, and Maryann Feldman (Oxford: Oxford University Press, 2000) 83–98; Spencer Glendon, *Urban Life Cycles,* working paper (Cambridge, MA: Harvard University, 1998); Curtis Simon, "Human Capital and Metropolitan Employment Growth," *Journal of Urban Economics,* 43, 1998: 223–43 provides empirical evidence of the association between human capital or talent and regional economic growth; see V.K. Mathur, "Human Capital-Based Strategy for Regional Economic Development," *Economic Development Quarterly* 13, 3, 1999: 203–16 for a review.

5. Edward Glaeser, J. Kolko, and A. Saiz, "Consumer City," *Journal of Economic Geography* 1 (2001): 27–50; Richard Lloyd, "Digital Bohemia: New Media Enterprises in Chicago's Wicker Park," paper presented at the annual meeting of the American Sociological Association, August 2001, Anaheim, California; Richard Lloyd and Terry Clark, "The City as Entertainment Machine," in *Research in Urban Sociology,* Vol. 6, *Critical Perspectives on Urban Redevelopment,* ed. Kevin Fox Gatham, 2001, 357–78. Oxford: JAI/Elsevier.

6. V.K. Mathur, "Human Capital-Based Strategy for Regional Economic Development," *Economic Development Quarterly* 13, 3, 1999: 203–16; G.H. Hanson, "Firms, Workers,

and the Geographic Concentration of Economic Activity," in *The Oxford Handbook of Economic Geography*, ed. Gordon Clark, Meric Gertler, and Maryann Feldman (Oxford: Oxford University Press, 2000), 477–94.

7. Jane Jacobs, *The Death and Life of Great American Cities* (New York: Random House, 1961) and *The Economy of Cities* (New York: Random House, 1969).

8. Edwin Ullman, "Regional Development and the Geography of Concentration," *Papers and Proceedings of the Regional Science Association*, 4, 1958: 179–98.

9. A. E. Andersson, "Creativity and Regional Development," *Papers of the Regional Science Association*, 56 (1985): 5–20; Pierre Desroshers, "Diversity, Human Creativity, and Technological Innovation," *Growth and Change* 32, 2001.

10. Paul Romer, "Endogenous Technological Change," *Journal of Political Economy*, 98, 5, 1990: S71–S102.

11. Robert Lucas, Jr., "On the Mechanics of Economic Development," *Journal of Monetary Economics*, 22, 1988: 1–42.

12. J. Eaton, and Z. Eckstein, "Cities and Growth: Theory and Evidence from France and Japan," *Regional Science and Urban Economics*, 27, 4–5, 1997: 443–74; D. Black and V. Henderson, "A Theory of Urban Growth," *Journal of Political Economy*, 107, 2, 1998: 252–84.

13. J. E. Rauch, "Productivity Gains from Geographic Concentrations of Human Capital: Evidence from Cities," *Journal of Urban Economics*, 34, 1993: 380–400.

14. Edward Glaeser, J. A. Sheinkman, and A. Sheifer, "Economic Growth in a Cross-Section of Cities," *Journal of Monetary Economics* 36, 1995: 117–43.

15. Curtis Simon and C. Nardinelli, "The Talk of the Town: Human Capital, Information and the Growth of English Cities, 1861–1961," *Explorations in Economic History*, 33, 3, 1996: 384–413.

16. Edward Glaeser, "The New Economics of Urban and Regional Growth," in *The Oxford Handbook of Economic Geography*, ed. Gordon Clark, Meric Gertler, and Maryann Feldman (Oxford: Oxford University Press, 2000), 83–98.

17. Curtis Simon, "Human Capital and Metropolitan Employment Growth," *Journal of Urban Economics*, 43, 1998: 223–43; Spencer Glendon, "Urban Life Cycles," Working paper (Cambridge, MA: Harvard University, 1998).

18. Paul Gottlieb, "Residential Amenities, Firm Location and Economic Development," *Urban Studies*, 32: 1995, 1413–36.

19. Richard Lloyd, and Terry Clark. "The City as Entertainment Machine," in *Research in Urban Sociology*, vol. 6, *Critical Perspectives on Urban Redevelopment*, ed. Kevin Fox Gatham, (2001) 357–78. Oxford: JAI/Elsevier; Lloyd, R. "Digital Bohemia: New Media Enterprises in Chicago's Wicker Park," paper presented at the annual meeting of the American Sociological Association, August 2001, Anaheim, California.

20. Joel Kotkin, *The New Geography* (New York: Random House, 2000.)

21. Edward Glaeser, J. Kolko, and A. Saiz, "Consumer City," *Journal of Economic Geography*, 1, 2001: 27–50.

22. Edward Glaeser, *The Future of Urban Research: Nonmarket Interactions* (Washington, D.C.: Brookings Institution, 1999).

23. John Quigley, "Urban Diversity and Economic Growth," *Journal of Economic Perspectives*, 12, 2, 1998: 127–38.

24. Jane Jacobs, *The Death and Life of Great American Cities* (New York: Random House, 1961).

25. Pierre Desroshers, "Diversity, Human Creativity, and Technological Innovation," *Growth and Change*, 32, 2001.

26. Pascal Zachary, *The Global Me: New Cosmopolitans and the Competitive Edge—Picking Globalism's Winners and Losers* (New York: Perseus Books, 2000).

27. Annalee Saxenian, *Silicon Valley's New Immigrant Entrepreneurs* (Berkeley, California: Public Policy Institute of California, 1999).1

28. Qualitative research, including interviews and focus groups, was initially conducted to better understand the structure and mechanics of these relationships and to generate testable hypothesis. Unstructured, open-ended interviews were conducted with more than 100 people who were making, or had recently made, location decisions. Structured focus groups were conducted to further assess the factors involved in personal location decisions. The original focus groups were conducted in March 1999 in Pittsburgh, with the assistance of a professional focus group organization. The author and the research team worked together with the focus group organization to screen focus group participants and develop the instrument.

29. The focus groups took place over the course of a week and were conducted in a specialized facility with a one-way mirror for observation.

30. R. Boyer, and D. Savageau, 1989. Places Rated Almanac: Your Guide to Finding the Best Places to Live in North America (New York: Prentice-Hall Travel).

31. Daniel Black, Gary Gates, Seth Sanders, and Lowell Taylor, Demographics of the Gay and Lesbian Population in the United States: Evidence from Available Systematic Data Sources. *Demography*, 73 (2), 2000: 139–54 for a discussion of this measure.

32. S. Rosen, "Hedonic Prices and Implicit Markets: Product Differentiation in Pure Competition," *Journal of Political Economy*, 82, 1974: 34–55.

33. Ross Devol, P. Wong, J. Catapano, G. Robitshek. 1999, *America's High-Tech Economy: Growth, Development, and Risks for Metropolitan Areas*, Milken Institute (Santa Monica, CA.)

34. The results generated R-squared values between 0.65 and 0.75.

35. At the 0.001 level.

36. At the 0.10 level.

37. The adjusted R-squared values for these models range from 0.64 to 0.68.

38. The adjusted R-squared for this model is 0.635.

39. First, talent is strongly associated with high-technology industry: the direct effect of talent on high-technology industry location is 0.42. Second, diversity is associated both with talent and high-technology industry: The direct effect of diversity on talent is 0.59. Diversity also works indirectly on high-technology industry via its effect on talent. This indirect effect is 0.25. This indirect effect is calculated by multiplying the effect of diversity on talent (0.59) and the effect of talent on high-technology industry (0.42.) In addition, diversity has a direct effect on high-technology industry of 0.35. When combined, the total effect of diversity on high-technology industry is 0.60. Third, the path analysis suggests that the effects of other variables, such as coolness or other amenity measures, are weak and frequently negative (not shown in Figure 4.6). For example, coolness has a weak positive effect (0.15) on talent but a negative effect (−0.024) on high-technology industry. Cultural amenities have a weak positive effect on both talent (0.14) and high-technology industry (0.16). Recreational amenities have a weak negative effect (−0.34) on talent and a weak positive effect (0.05) on high-technology industry. Climate has a weak negative effect (−0.17) on talent and a small positive effect (0.20) on high-technology industry.

40. For example, coolness has a weak positive effect on talent but a negative effect on high-technology industry. Cultural amenities have a weak positive effect on both talent and high-technology industry. Recreational amenities have a weak negative effect on talent and a weak positive effect on high-technology industry. Climate has a weak negative effect on talent and a small positive effect on high-technology industry.

41. Curtis Simon, "Human capital and metropolitan employment growth." *Journal of Urban Economics* 43 (1998): 223–43.

42. The correlation coefficient between talent and per-capita income level (1997) is 0.588. More interesting, however, is the strong positive correlation between income and the diversity index (0.498).
43. The adjusted R-squared values for these models are 0.57 and 0.65, respectively.
44. The correlation coefficient for absolute income change (1991–1997) and talent (1990) is 0.337. That is, the level of talent in 1990 predicts the absolute dollar change in income between 1991 and 1997. The results of the regression analysis suggest that this relationship is robust (see Table 4.5). The dependent variable in the model is absolute change in income (1991–1997), and the independent variables are talent, diversity, high-technology industry, and median house-value. The adjusted R-squared value for the model is 0.225. Talent is the only variable in the model that is positively and significantly associated with income change.
45. Here several findings are of note. First, talent has a direct effect on income (0.41) as well as a direct effect on high-technology location (0.42). This is greater than the direct effect of high-technology industry on income (0.35). The estimated total effect of talent on income is 0.56. Furthermore, while diversity has no direct effect on income, it has a substantial indirect effect. This analysis indicates that diversity works indirectly on income through two additional paths. Working through high-technology industry, the indirect effect of diversity on income is 0.12. Working indirectly through talent and then high-technology industry, the indirect effect of diversity on income is 0.24. The estimated total effect of diversity on income is 0.37.

Chapter 5

1. Robert Park, (orig. 1915), "The City: Suggestions for the Investigation of Human Behavior," *The Subcultures Reader*, eds., Ken Gelder and Sarah Thornton (New York: Routledge, 1997).
2. Caesar Grana, *Bohemian Versus Bourgeois: French Society and the French Man of Letters in the Nineteenth Century* (New York: Basic Books, 1964).
3. David Brooks, *Bobos in Paradise: The New Upper Class and How They Got There* (New York: Simon and Schuster, 2000).
4. Jane Jacobs, *The Death and Life of Great American Cities* (New York: Random House, 1961).
5. Neil Smith, *The New Urban Frontier: Gentrification and the Revanchist City* (New York: Routledge. 1996.)
6. Terry Clark, and Richard Lloyd. "The Entertainment Machine." (Chicago: University of Chicago).
7. New England Council. *The Creative Economy Initiative: The Roe of the Arts ad Culture in New England's Economic Competitiveness.* (Boston: New England Council, July 2000).
8. Grana, *Bohemian Versus Bourgeois* (New York: Basic Books 1964).
9. Daniel Bell, *"The Cultural Contradictions of Capitalism"* (New York: Basic Books 1976).
10. Ibid.
11. John Seabrook, *No Brow: The Culture of Marketing, the Marketing of Culture* (New York: Alfred A. Knopf 2000).
12. David Brooks, *Bobos in Paradise: The New Upper Class and How They Got There* (New York: Simon and Schuster 2000).
13. Tom Frank, *The Conquest of Cool: Business Culture, Counterculture, and the Rise of Hip Consumerism* (Chicago: University of Chicago Press 1997).
14. Robert Park, (orig. 1915) "The City: Suggestions for the Investigation of Human Behavior," *The Subcultures Reader*, eds. Ken Gelder and Sarah Thornton (New York: Routledge, 1997).

15. Jane Jacobs, *The Death and Life of Great American Cities* (New York: Random House 1961).

16. John Hannigan, *The Fantasy City: Pleasure and Profit in the Postmodern Metropolis.* (London: Routledge 1998).

17. Terry Clark and Richard Lloyd, *The Entertainment Machine* (Chicago: University of Chicago 2000).

18. Joel Kotkin, *The New Geography: How the Digital Revolution is Reshaping the American Landscape* (New York: Random House 2000).

19. Unstructured open-ended interviews were conducted with more than 100 people who were making, or had recently made, location decisions. Structured focus groups were conducted with the assistance of a professional focus group organization to further assess the factors involved in personal location decisions.

20. Boyer and Savegeau, *Places Rated Almanac*, 1989.

21. The correlation is 0.541 and is significant at the 0.01 level.

22. The correlation is 0.512 and is also significant at the 0.01 level.

23. The correlation between the Bohemian Index and the Talent Index is 0.553 and is positive at the 0.01 level.

24. The correlation between the Bohemian Index and the Gay Index is 0.60. The correlation between the Bohemian Index and the Melting Pot Index is 0.505. Both are significant at the 0.01 level.

25. The results of the various models generated adjusted R-squared values that are above 0.7, suggesting a robust and positive relationship.

26. The correlation is 0.65 and is significant at the 0.01 level.

27. The various models generated adjusted R-squared values that hover around 0.6 or slightly better.

Chapter 6

1. Richard Lucas, "On the Mechanics of Economic Development," *Journal of Monetary Economics*, 1988: 38–9. Lucas says: "If we postulate only the usual list of economic forces, cities should fly apart. The theory of production contains nothing to hold a city together. A city is simply a collection of factors of production—capital, people, and land—and land is always far cheaper outside cities than inside . . . It seems to me that the *force* we need to postulate account for the central role of cities in economic life is of exactly the same character as the *external human capital* . . . What can people be paying Manhattan or downtown Chicago rents for, if not for being near other people?"

2. Edward Glaeser, 'The New Economics of Urban and Regional Growth," in *The Oxford Handbook of Economic Geography*, ed. Gordon Clark, Meric Gertler, and Maryann Feldmen, (Oxford: Oxford University Press, 2000), 83–98; Glaeser, "Are Cities Dying?" *Journal of Economic Perspectives*, 12, 1998, 139–160; Glaesar, "Learning in Cities," NBER working paper, 6271, 1997; Edward Glaeser, J.A. Sheinkman, and A. Sheifer, "Economic Growth in a Cross-Section of Cities," *Journal of Monetary Economics*, 36, (1995), 117–143.

3. The analysis indicated a Pearson correlation between the Milken Tech Pole and the population with a college degree at 0.72. The Spearman rank order correlation was 0.60—that is the relationship between the rank number of a region on the Tech-Pole and the rank on the percentage of the population with a BA or above. Interestingly, talent explains more than 50 percent of the variation in high-technology concentration.

4. E. G. Chambers et al., "The War for Talent," *The McKinsey Quarterly*, 3, 1998.

5. We combine any MSAs that are also part of a Consolidated Meropolitan Statistical Area (CMSA) as defined by the U.S. Census Bureau. As a result, the following areas are constituted as a single metropolitan area:

San Francisco: San Francisco, Oakland, San Jose
Los Angeles: Los Angeles, Anaheim, Riverside
Miami: Miami, Fort Lauderdale
New York: New York, Bergen County, Newark, Middlesex County, Nassau County, Suffolk County, Monmouth County

6. The Census Bureau releases two public-use samples of decennial census person-level data, the 1 percent and 5 percent PUMS. The 5 percent PUMS is a representative sample (3 in 10) drawn from the 1 in 6 sample of people who filled out a census long-form, which amounts to 5 percent of the U.S. population or approximately 12 million observations. The sample is representative of the entire U.S. population and also is considered representative within metropolitan statistical areas, the unit of analysis utilized for this work.

7. Daniel Black, Gary Gates, Seth Sanders, and Lowell Taylor, "Demographics of the Gay and Lesbian Population in the United States: Evidence from Available Systematic Data Sources," *Demography*, 37: 2, 2000, 139–154. They demonstrate that unmarried same-sex partners in the Census are comprised primarily of gay and lesbian couples.

8. Ross DeVol, P. Wong, J. Catapano, and G. Robitshek, *America's High-Tech Economy: Growth, Development, and Risks for Metropolitan Areas*, (Milken Institute. 1999)

9. DeVol et al., 1999.

10. In addition to statistical research on the 50 metropolitan areas, the study was informed by interviews, focus groups, and case studies the authors have conducted separately or together over the past several years.

11. A number of reasons exist why this conclusion makes sense. Gay males are less likely to have children. In addition, if they couple with another male, their household income will be on average higher than the income of male/female households because males on average earn more than females in our economy. With no children in the household and relatively high incomes, gay couples can devote larger portions of their income to the purchase and development of amenities. See Daniel Black, Gary Gates, Seth Sanders, Lowell Taylor, "Why Do Gay Men Live in San Francisco," *Journal of Urban Economics*, 2001. Research has shown that gay male couples live in some of America's most sought after urban areas and are more likely to live in distressed areas within cities and gentrify their surroundings more than any other household type. See Gary Gates, *Essays on the Demographics and Location Patterns of Coupled Gay Men*, unpublished doctoral dissertation (H. John Heinz III School of Public Policy and Management, Carnegie Mellon University, 2000).

12. Several cautions must be noted regarding the Census data and gays and lesbians. We are measuring only individuals in same-sex unmarried partner relationships. As such, these figures do not take into account nonpartnered gays. In addition, we estimate that the Census only captured approximately 35 percent of all gay/lesbian partnerships. Black et al., "Demographics of the Gay and Lesbian Population in the United States."

13. The Pearson correlation between the Gay Index and the Tech-Pole index was 0.77 while the Spearman rank-order correlation was 0.60 (both are significant at the 0.001 level). The growth index measures change in high-tech output within metropolitan areas from 1990 to 1998 relative to national change in output during the same period.

14. The high correlation observed between the gay concentration and the high-technology index could in part be a result of a limited sample of the 50 largest metropolitan areas in the country. Therefore, further studies examined if this positive association remains when a broader cross-section of metropolitan areas is utilized. Indeed, while the correlation does weaken when 242 metropolitan statistical areas are examined, it is still positive and significant at 0.23.

15. The overall F-statistic for the model is also only signal at the 0.07 level. This means that the total predictive power of the combined variables is significant, but somewhat

weak. There is also a strong relationship between the concentration of gays in a metropolitan area and other measures of diversity, notably the percent of foreign-born residents: San Francisco, Washington, D.C., and Los Angeles all ranked highly. These results reiterate the impact of diversity on a broad section of society. Low barriers to entry seem to be good for the whole economy, not just high-skilled labor

16. The only qualitative difference was that the Pearson correlation between percent college graduate and the Tech-Pole index was slightly higher than the same correlation with the gay index. However, the Spearman rank order correlation with the Tech-Pole index was higher for the Gay Index.

17. One question raised by this strong connection between gays and high-technology is the extent to which gays and lesbians are overrepresented in the industry. If gays and lesbians make up large fractions of this industry, then it could be that the location of high-technology firms brings about a larger concentration of gays in a region. To look at this, we analyzed 1990 Census data to assess the extent to which gays and lesbians are overrepresented in some high-technology fields and industries. Gay men are about 1.3 times more likely to be scientists and engineers than the population in general. Lesbians are as likely as the rest of the population to be in these occupations. If the gay men and lesbians are combined, the result shows that they are 1.2 times more likely than the population to be scientists and engineers. We also examined those employed by the computer and data-processing services industry: Gay men are 2.3 times, and lesbians are 1.3 times, more likely than the population to be employed in this industry. Together, gays and lesbians are 1.9 times more likely than the population to be employed in the computer services industry. While some of the correlation between gays and high-technology might result from their overrepresentation in the industry, it seems difficult to explain how their overrepresentation would predict growth. To do so would be to suggest that that gays and lesbians are somehow on average more productive or entrepreneurial than their heterosexual counterparts.

18. Originally, we undertook a series of analyses using various measures of amenities. We looked at things like climate, professional sports, arts and culture, and many others. In most of this work, we found only a loose relationship between amenities, talent, and technology. A large part of the reason, we came to believe, was due to the measures themselves. They were based on combinations of different factors and were not very consistent or reliable. And many of the things we would have liked to measure—such as a city's music or art scene were simply unavailable.

19. The two measures are correlated at 0.62 using a Pearson correlation and 0.54 using a Spearman rank-order correlation. Both are significant at the 0.001 level.

20. While an association between the Bohemian index and the Tech-Pole index is observed, a similar connection between growth and this index is not noted. Alone, the Boho Index can explain nearly 38 percent of the variation in high-tech concentration. The combination of the Boho Index and our measure of talent account for nearly 60 percent of the high-tech concentration measure.

21. William Frey, and Ross DeVol, *America's Demography in the New Century: Aging Baby Boomers and New Immigrants as Major Players* (Santa Monica Milken Institute, March 2000).

22. See also John Quigley, "Urban Diversity and Economic Growth." *Journal of Economic Perspectives*, 12: 2, 1998: 127–138.

23. Annalee Saxenian, *Silicon Valley's New Immigrant Entrepreneurs* (Public Policy Institute of California, 1999).

24. The Pearson correlation between percent foreign born and the Tech-Pole index was 0.43 (significant at the 0.01 level) and the Spearman rank-order correlation with 0.48 (significant at the 0.001 level). We did not find a similar correlation with high-technology growth.

25. The Pearson correlation was −0.11 and the Spearman rank-order correlation was −0.20. Neither were statistically significant.
26. The Spearman rank order correlation between the Milken Tech-Pole and the composite diversity measure was 0.63. See Appendix B for other correlations.

INDEX